AF316700

GETTING MY
HAPPY
BACK

How to Think and What to Do When Body and Mind Collide

DR. RENÉE OSTERTAG
and
WILENE DUNN

Author Contacts
Dr. Renée Ostertag, renee@greentreemind.com
Wilene Dunn, wilene@writingthatbook.com

Published by WCD Publishing

ISBN (paperback): 979-8-8740-2582-3
ISBN (hardcover): 979-8-3484-7194-1

Edited by Shannon Dunn with Andrea Glass
Cover Design by Melanie Mitchell, Overall Productions and Elena Reznikova
Interior Layout and Design by DTPerfect Book Design

Contents

Author's Note

We want to emphasize that the phrase "getting my happy back" doesn't mean succumbing to toxic positivity or denying the unpleasant realities of life. We've all faced challenging and difficult experiences, and we understand putting icing on a burned cake doesn't make it edible.

Our intention is to share a message that combines science, personal stories and our own journeys through tough times. We've learned how to navigate through life experiences, acknowledge the impact they've had on our nervous systems, and muster the courage to find our way back to a life filled with vibrancy and pleasant sensations. We are hopeful this book offers you a pathway that can help you restore your authentic self, embracing all the colors, shapes, sizes, and flavors. Rediscover what sets you apart, allowing you to thrive and embrace life, even after facing its challenging phases.

It's important to recognize that you don't have to go through this process alone. We wrote this book together because no one is meant to face pain, stress and trauma on their own. Sometimes, we all need a hand to hold when things get scary, and we are here to support you through this message, as much or as little as you need. Remember, it's okay if holding hands isn't your thing—we get it.

The journey to Getting Your Happy Back may have unexpected twists and turns, but it can also be joyous and fulfilling. If anything in this book stirs up emotions that feel too overwhelming to handle alone, we encourage you to seek professional or community support. You deserve to have someone by your side through the tough times.

Throughout our writing journey, we confronted our old patterns of familiarity, which often led to anxiety, depression, panic, and stress. Breaking free from these patterns wasn't easy; it felt like going through withdrawal from an addictive substance. Thankfully, we had each other's understanding to ride the waves of discomfort as happiness began to build inside us. Learning to feel safe and okay with feeling safe and okay was a process, especially for those of us not used to such emotions. But remember, that's all part of the journey, and it's okay.

You might find yourself caught in patterns of toxic positivity, struggling with boundaries, people-pleasing, hyper-achieving, or other unhelpful strategies at the expense of your own well-being. As you begin to experience more happy feelings that naturally emerge as you leave your unhelpful patterns behind, you may experience some sabotage behaviors, outbursts, anger, sadness, depression, and all those chemicals flooding your nervous system as you discover a new version of you. The process of Getting Your Happy Back entails understanding how to navigate through fluctuations and harness their momentum.

Think of it like bowling—once you've learned how to bowl, your body and nervous system thankfully remember how to bowl. You wouldn't want to learn how to hold the ball, where to stand in the lane and release the ball over and over. Similarly, we have a supportive system that remembers how to handle trauma responses, but we also need to unlearn the behaviors, thoughts and chemicals associated with them. This book aims to help you become acutely aware of these repetitive responses and pave the way for a healthier and happier life.

We have gathered some key takeaways for you at the end of each chapter called Chapter Reflections. We find value in the belief that these reflections serve as an opportunity for you to incorporate cognitive learning into the practical arena of your life, ultimately assisting you to embrace authentic wholeness and achieve greater harmony.

So, as you dive into this book, remember that it's okay to feel awkward, uncomfortable or resistant to change. Embrace the journey, lean on support when necessary and persist through the challenges—because that's the pathway to Getting Your Happy Back!

Introduction

If you are reading this book, you want to improve your physical and mental health. So many people deal with inflammation, chronic pain, sadness, depression, and toxic stress. And we were (and sometimes still are!) some of those people. By learning to listen to our bodies and pay attention to our thoughts and the words we speak, we got our Happy back.

My name is Dr. Renée Ostertag, and I hold a Clinical Doctorate in Physical Therapy (DPT). I excel at scouring and metabolizing complex science, then delivering it in bite-sized pieces with real-life applications.

And I am Wilene Dunn, an entrepreneur, innovator and author focused on encouraging others to reach their full potential with professional and personal empowerment coaching.

Follow along as we support each other, exchange knowledge and share our experiences—both triumphs and failures—in our process of getting our Happy back. Ready?

DISCONNECTED
GRACE
POWERLESS
GRIT
TENSION
GOOD LUCK
CONTRACTION
STRESS VORTEX
FREEDOM
I think I can?
Not sure... scared...
and I need help.
This is hard...
but I'm doing it!
This is challenging...
and totally worth it.
I CAN'T
I CAN
I CHOOSE
PATH FOR EXPANSION AND GROWTH
greentree
mind
www.NS-Ninja.com

It's Not You — It's Your Nervous System

"It's not my fault, but it is now my responsibility."
DR. RENÉE OSTERTAG

First, we need to tell the truth. What we've been doing as a society at large to treat pain, stress and depression isn't working. People are getting worse—not better. As a society, we are becoming sicker—not healthier. Some research suggests that negative stress, pressure and anxiety are at all-time highs. For many, social and economic changes are occurring at a faster pace than the primitive parts of our nervous system can adjust and evolve. As Maxwell Maltz states, "Your nervous system cannot tell the difference between an actual experience and one that is vividly imagined."

We can influence the external events in our lives. We can shift our perceptions and understandings of them. We can adopt new skills, methods and techniques to navigate pain and change differently than we have before.

> **We can influence the external events in our lives. We can shift our perceptions and understandings of them.**

When I first met Renée, I was coming out of an emotionally distressing relationship. I could hardly move my body, bend or find any relief from the tension and stress I was experiencing. My office was upstairs, and I thought my body was going to break in half with every step. After sitting, standing seemed almost impossible. My neck hurt so badly, I was always stretching it from shoulder to shoulder, chin to chest searching for some relief, but nothing worked.

I had a massage thinking that if I could relieve the physical tension in my muscles, I would feel better. But the massage offered no relief. In fact, it was extremely painful.

I had been taking anti-inflammatories daily and began taking sleep aids to be comfortable enough to rest. My first session with Renée was a getting-to-know-you conversation, which made a general impact on how I was feeling. As I continued, I learned that expression and being emphatically listened to about what was going on with me began to relieve some of the stiffness and pain.

An initial lesson I learned was to listen in a new way, beyond the pain and how to get past the physical circuits of Fight, Flight and Freeze. These are physiological defense mechanisms that any mammal will use when it perceives a potential or actual threat to its survival. The difference between humans and other mammals is that our fight/flight/freeze response can be triggered by psychological fears or perceived threats, in addition to objectively true environmental dangers (external or internal environment). What was my body wanting to tell me by causing me so much agony?

My pain was worse when I experienced any kind of work stress or even being in a room where I had experienced trauma during my relationship. The stress of change was producing paralyzing pain. I remember saying, "I actually thought it was normal to feel aches and pain in my body." Persistent body pain does not have to be a normal part of our everyday lives that we just need to get used to!

I discovered my coping mechanism was freeze. I experienced my circuits of freeze by sleeping excessively. My body felt locked up—frozen.

A lot of my physical pain was an emotional trauma response, not just from the current relationship issue but from an early childhood experience when freeze became my nervous system's default mode network response. Thankfully, instead of beating myself up, I learned from Renée that it wasn't my fault. Freeze is a healthy and biologically appropriate response to overwhelming life events. It's a very common, normal and natural response for children whose nervous systems haven't yet fully matured.

I (Renée) have been in Physical Therapy since 2000 and I have noticed significant emphasis on treating symptoms and physical pain, as though body tissues exist in a vacuum and aren't related to our thinking, feeling, life experiences, and environments. The health care system focuses on finding what's wrong, diagnosing it, then trying to fix it. My profession historically tries to fix it through a primarily bottom-up approach of restoring muscle flexibility, strength, power, and physical function. The psychotherapy field has traditionally focused on a more top-down approach, trying to "fix what's broken" through adjusting thinking, feeling and behavior strategies. None of these tunnel-vision approaches are able to fully incorporate the totality of what is going on with a whole human being and their persistent pain. The medical system isn't successful at finding and fixing, because chronic pain and suffering don't live in one isolated place inside of you.

Persistent health issues are widespread, elusive and can live inside of you in a way that touches everything about you. There's a hidden, physical component that involves how the nervous system perceives life events as threatening and can create incomplete stress responses. These get stored in the body, which can leave some of us with years of nagging pain even after a physical injury has healed or the emotionally stressing event has passed. As a licensed, practicing physical therapist (and mental health therapist) with decades in the field, I (Renée) am an expert at navigating the confusing terrain between mind and body. I am a proud Nervous System Ninja that loves supporting others to confidently become the same. I stand hopeful and relieved that I can tell you there is a way for you to become empowered, to restore a sense of control in your life, and to gain greater freedom from the grip that pain can have on your quality of life. You too can become a Nervous System Ninja!

Science tells us that every experience of pain has three dimensions to it: physical, emotional and social. Many patients have reinforced this scientific understanding of pain for me—the emotional state and social environments of our lives have a very real biological and chemical effect on our pain. Emotions and environments can turn the volume on our pain up or down. Wilene learned this when she learned to listen to the stiffness and pain with a new understanding of the 3D nature of pain. She began to notice that her stiffness and pain would resurface when she was unhappy.

Nancy, for example, a 53-year-old psychologist who initially reported that her back just didn't like sitting learned to recognize that her back didn't actually hurt during all sitting across the spectrum of her entire life. Through our work, she discovered she didn't have back pain when she was sitting at her office (doing work she loved), which served as credible evidence for her that her back didn't always hurt while sitting. She developed pattern recognition around her back pain and its behaviors. With time, Nancy discovered she didn't actually have back pain when sitting and feeling content. She noticed she experienced back pain when she was unhappy, such as sitting at a hot afternoon baseball game or in a wet chair at a stubborn and demanding bride's wedding who insisted the ceremony remain outdoors despite a torrential rainstorm. Nancy was surprised that the story "my back just doesn't like sitting" wasn't true, because the objective truth was that she could sit at times without any discomfort while working. Through our curious inquiry, she discovered that her back could indeed tolerate sitting. "It was just trying to tell me that I'm not happy!"

I learned to see there was an underlying positive intention of the pain she was experiencing. Wilene realized her pain was acting as an alarm system to notify her of subconscious threats and fears, and that pain was her body's way of trying to help her move from a place of unhappiness to a better place.

The people I've worked with over the past 20 years in my professional arena have been fantastic teachers for me. In many ways, they've taught me what I know about how to regulate a nervous system. I know what I know, as a result of witnessing many people getting to know what works, what doesn't, why, when, and how. I love, appreciate and respect the people I've worked with. They are courageous in letting themselves be seen in their struggles and challenges of life. It can be difficult to admit weakness, pain, struggle, and the imperfections in the landscape of life's messiness as a human being.

I now would like to be brave and do some courageous truth telling here: My work has been difficult for me. I've witnessed a lot of suffering and was living in my own suffering while doing so. I was suffering with my own mental and physical health challenges. I had years of PTSD, anxiety, depression, debilitating back pain, and plaguing irritable bowel syndrome. To make it worse, as a healthcare provider, I had a limited perspective and narrow understanding of these painful experiences in my life.

My one-dimensional thinking had me believing the back pain radiating down my legs creating weakness and cauda equina symptoms (a condition of pinched nerves in the back that affect bowel, bladder and sexual function, which traditional training considers a surgical emergency) was coming entirely from the bulging discs pinching my L4/5 and L5/S1 nerve roots. This is a reasonable and rational belief, according to my training and traditional western medical indoctrination.

This same one-dimensional thinking in my back pain was used to try and deal with my irritable bowel syndrome diagnosis. I thought the constant bloating, cycling of constipation, diarrhea, and super inconvenient fecal urgency were all coming from my broken and busted bowels (leaky gut syndrome), and I'd just need to limit my gluten and dairy intake for the rest of my life. Again, these are not unreasonable and are completely understandable thought processes, given the current teachings and training. My experience suggests that food limiting is effective but does not solve the entire problem and only shows a partial picture of a greater whole. My biggest suffering came from the mistake in my thinking that my partial perspective was the whole story.

Life can be a tough teacher—it gives you the test first and the lesson after. And pain is a profound vehicle for learning.

At the time of this writing, I've had over 30,000 patient encounters in my career and will continue to experience each of them as they endure some sort of challenging life lessons through pain and/or suffering. I've had to learn these tough life lessons myself. The evidence seems to suggest that none of us get out of here alive without some sections of our lives that include pain, suffering and things that suck.

We resist them. That is natural! We are wired to move away from a hot stove—it's a survival instinct. But if our survival instincts are the only governing force guiding our nervous system, we will surely suffer. Suffering is resisting what is.

When I was 11 years old, my beloved, healthy, active, and lively mother had a sudden brain aneurysm at age 47 and tragically left the house for the last time in an ambulance. My father, who I was deathly afraid of, was deeply depressed for years afterward. The feeling of my safe childhood home had shifted from an alive, bustling grand central station filled with vitality into a place where I felt trapped in a desolate and dark castle dungeon. Around the same time, my three older sisters all left home. Throughout my formative years, from 11 to 18, I felt abandoned by the four women of my core family and kept the disconnected company of my emotionally struggling father. I felt trapped in the discomfort of a lonely home and a frozen father. It didn't help that his father dropped dead of a stroke in front of him when my dad was 15. Generational trauma, anyone? I didn't want any of that, nor did my father. It sucked for both of us.

I didn't have the skills or tools to deal with it. I did the best I could and kept pushing through being the brave little soldier. This can be called resilience, and it is. But, unbeknownst to me, a deep underground layer of my nervous system (affecting my back, bowels and mental health) got stuck in a fight/flight/freeze response from all that shock and repetitive stress and trauma of not feeling safe, seen or heard by my dad. Well, there was our awesome cat, with his awesome Swiss name—Buzi. That cat got me through some rough times!

Wilene identified the default network mode of her nervous system in blue or freeze. I identified in red or a fight/flight response. When I am afraid and don't know it, I go into a mode of fight or flight. When Wilene is afraid and doesn't know it, she goes into freeze mode. These aren't character flaws—they are biology.

What is your default network mode?

It took me years to figure out that my health challenges (anxiety, gut, back, neck, adrenal fatigue, hypertension, cancer scares—yep, plural) were connected to incomplete stress response cycles in the circuits of my subconscious nervous system.

We don't like difficult health challenges, so we resist them. As I've helped patients learn how to work with and utilize body and mind to overcome crippling pain and release toxic stress, I've learned it myself. I remember a crisis point many years ago when I lay in bed staring blankly at the bedroom doorknob. I'd been trying to manage my incapacitating back pain for two weeks. I had just finished studying with pain specialists in Australia—tissues heal, we can control our pain— but those teachings failed me.

Catastrophic thinking began to take hold. What would I do? How could I help my patients heal if I couldn't even heal myself? Once a nationally ranked college athlete in the heptathlon, I now could barely move. Stretching my back, I felt a tear. Suddenly, I was gripped by the very thing I had spent so much of my life learning to heal. I felt paralyzed. Bedridden, I began to wonder what would happen to me if I could no longer work. The pain began to radiate from my back down my legs. How would I have a career? Would I become homeless? I was living in a foreign country. I might have to rely on my father for money—the same person I had so many issues with following my mom's death. My tragic past had become my tormented present. My suffering present was a reflection of how my nervous system remembered my painful past. This is a vicious cycle that kept catastrophic thoughts cascading through my mind and worsening the sciatic pain in my legs. In the end, I persevered and was able to claim my life back. My past, I learned, did not have to control my future or my body.

Yes, we have been there, in our own version of where you might be right now. We found a way through, and we are offering our lessons to you. We have trained our bodies to work with our minds to allow healing to occur. As we recognize fear and anger showing up in our bodies, we developed the courage to confront unpleasant emotions and sensations. Ultimately, we needed to stop ignoring things that kept the pain cycling through us. There could be an unhelpful old program running inside of you.

Life experiences can leave skid marks on your nervous system and ugly tracks of unresolved emotions. We discovered more strategies besides avoiding and repressing inconvenient and uncomfortable body signals to get through the day and so can you.

We are here to share with you that Healing Happens. It's possible for us all to find freedom from perpetuating physical pain and mental distress—and that includes you! We point to our experience, Wilene's coaching clients and decades of Renée's experiences with patients. But let's not stop there. It's time to look at the credible evidence of science to support us in illuminating a path that shows you a way.

Here is what science tells us: Pain is a complex phenomenon, a construct of consciousness, that is widely misunderstood. There are ways out of pain, but we have been focusing on the wrong things as we try to rid ourselves of pain. The medical profession has not been paying enough attention to how the nervous system processes injury, disease, hurt, pain, threat, and emotions. Yes, acute pain shocks us when we injure ourselves by breaking a bone, burning ouselves or when we step on a nail. It's supposed to. That is how our species has survived. Without pain, we would not be biologically motivated to change our behavior and move toward protection and safety that allows us to continue to live. Without the pain of a broken arm, we would not seek the treatment and cast that helps it heal. That's the thing we have seemingly forgotten: Healing Happens. Tissues heal. The broken bone does get repaired. Damage to the tissue can go away. The acute blow to the anatomical structure does damage, and then that anatomical damage heals. That is what nature and biology can do: Facilitate healing!

Science shows us that healing happens. Muscle strains likely take two to three weeks to heal. Bulging discs in the back reabsorb and clear over time, according to studies. Arthritis is normal, like wrinkles on the inside, and need not create pain—the science proves it. Yet sadly, many don't experience the natural mechanisms of healing. Even though tissue healing is a biological process that occurs naturally, pain persists for many.

While tissues can heal from damage, the nerves and brain that intend to protect and keep the human safe can get stuck in a misfiring electrical-chemical pattern. This is not unlike an overly sensitive electrical wiring system in a house that sends the alarm every time a leaf blows on the porch, instead of when a robber tries to break in. This process can be called hyperalgesia or allodynia. For many with persistent health issues, this sensitized and protective nervous system can continually communicate that the body remains under threat, even when there is no objective danger present in any given moment. This electrical-chemical system firing can cause sensations of pain and discomfort that are very real, can spread and be experienced throughout the body.

The more time has passed between the original injury that damaged tissue in the body (or emotional damage to the psyche), the less reliable pain is in terms of assessing actual tissue damage. The concrete examples of structural damage we keep trying to find to explain long-term pain are of limited use. We have not been paying enough attention to the implication of neurological aspects that have guided our survival as a species. Fear, emotion and past trauma can be an overlooked driving force creating widespread, ongoing pain in both body and mind.

CHAPTER REFLECTIONS

- **Trust in the body's capacity to heal.** What are ways that you can repair, rebuild and restore trust within yourself and relationship to your body?
- **Be patient and persistent.** Celebrate a time in your life when patience was beneficial.
- **Listen to your body.** Respond differently to sensation; find your breath before getting swept away with negative feelings.
- **Avoid one-dimensional thinking.** When you experience an unpleasant sensation, stay curious about what's happening physically, emotionally and socially.

CHAPTER TWO

Perception and Your Nervous System

*"The eye sees only what the mind
is prepared to comprehend."*
ROBERTSON DAVIES

Being restored to a life of greater ease, flow and dynamic equilibrium can be available for you. Viktor Frankl, a Jewish-Austrian physician and author of *Man's Search for Meaning*, teaches us through his lived experiences in a Nazi concentration camp that a life with moments of peace, joy, purpose, meaning, and love is available to us all, every day. We figure if he can find peace in a concentration camp, we can find peace amidst our struggles, pains and challenging life circumstances.

Being locked up in a state of persistent pain (mind or body) doesn't have to be permanent or indefinite. It's not normal, natural or healthy for you to remain locked up in pain. A human system's original design has built-in mechanisms for healing. We come factory installed to recover from hard things! You may fear that depression, anxiety, money problems, health issues, relationship challenges, and ongoing pain have become your fate, but that doesn't have to be the case.

**We come factory installed to
recover from hard things!**

Unfortunately, there is no magic pill. There is no single procedure or silver bullet that will fix it all for you in one fell swoop. There is no prescription or surgery that will rescue you from the necessary work to experience change in your life. *The only magic that will come to you, will do so because you take a stand, make a choice, and decide to take action—repeatedly.* Just one bicep curl doesn't give you bigger biceps! You are ultimately the best one to reorient your body and mind through disciplined, consistent practice.

In our discussion about leading a fulfilling and happy life, I (Wilene) wanted to share my journey of regaining my sense of happiness. Pain, whether physical or emotional, can significantly hinder our well-being. There are numerous factors that contribute to pain, physical injuries, mental struggles, and old programming. I want to emphasize the importance of our thoughts and words in shaping our experiences and how they played a role in my pain.

For example, I was feeling very stressed with the change of life circumstances when my partner moved out. Suddenly, I was solely accountable for maintaining the house, six dogs and all the financial responsibility that came with that change. My sense of overwhelm was driving me to talk extensively about the conditions during this adjustment period. I didn't realize the way I was sharing the story was actually reinforcing how the stress lived in my nervous system. Renée made me aware that when I spoke of the stressful concerns, my neck and shoulders would tense and my voice changed to a rapid, louder and higher pitch (a very normal, common stress response). I had no idea that each time I spoke of the stress in this tense way, that I was actually strengthening how the stressful circuits lived in my body. The story was reinforcing the nervous system loop to keep my physical and emotional pain in place.

Renée provided a safe environment for me, and together, we achieved co-regulation of our nervous systems. As we continued in this transformative dialogue, I could share more of my worries and not feel so alone and overwhelmed with them, which enabled my creative brain to come back online. This allowed me to generate new languaging around how that situation felt and begin affirming what I wanted. Telling the truth and being empathically witnessed allowed us to explore new levels of safety within my body. As I accessed each new level, I was able to confront and heal from past experiences and ingrained behavior patterns by perceiving and speaking about them differently.

This transformation in perspective led to changes in both my physical sensations and my overall sense of well-being.

You might wonder if simply altering your thoughts and establishing a shared connection of safety is enough to truly impact the pain you experience. Drawing from the evidence of my own journey, it's a necessary part of healing. I can assure you that it is indeed possible to heal, and it involves all levels of your being: How you think, feel, behave, move, communicate, practice, and live. If I could achieve this transformation, it's likely within reach for you as well.

To begin my healing process, the initial step was finding a safe space to express my emotions and connect with someone who would genuinely listen and empathize. From there, I started learning simple exercises to promote physical and emotional healing (many of these are on Renée's YouTube Channel **https://www.youtube.com/ @nervoussystemninja**). I stayed committed to my mindful practice of awareness of my thoughts and language, because those are also crucial pieces to getting my happy back.

Kate, a 26-year-old personal trainer, came to me with neck pain and anxiety from a car accident three years earlier. We discovered her fear of paralysis was rooted in words from the ER doctor. Those words became her reality, causing persistent pain and anxiety. Her nervous system held onto these words, causing ongoing discomfort despite healing. We realized harmful language, whether from others or ourselves, can deeply impact our bodies. But the good news is, once aware, we can change it. By revisiting the accident logically, acknowledging her healed state and reframing her understanding, Kate began to see her fear wasn't current or valid. This shift reduced her fear, enabling her to move more freely within months, even though the pain didn't vanish completely. Pain, often tied to fear or perceived danger, can be altered by changing our language and perception.

Kate's story teaches us the power of language in shaping our physical experiences. By understanding this influence and consciously shifting our words, we can alleviate unnecessary pain and fear, freeing ourselves from the limitations they impose. Kate heard the words of the doctor and those words became her lived experience.

I (Wilene) did the same. I became aware of my frequent repetition of stressors in a tense, tight body. Once I was aware, I could shift to using empowering language ("I can," instead of "I can't") in a more relaxed body. Instead of, "This sucks," it sounded more like, "This sucks, and it'll be okay. I can figure this out."

What are some words that you often use when it comes to talking about your current challenges? What language do you use in your daily life that is potentially threatening, scary or fear-based? What words do you hold that aren't helpful for you? What words have you been told that frighten and haunt you? For example, "I have a bad back," can be replaced with, "My back is in a healing process." Or "I'm an anxious person," can be changed to, "I'm a person that experiences anxiety more than I want to right now."

It's worth running an experiment for yourself. Spend 2-3 days and intentionally notice the language you use automatically as you speak to yourself. When you drop your phone or stub your toe, do you call yourself stupid or clumsy? Do your words reinforce an identity of being dumb? Do the things you say to yourself inadvertently strengthen a belief that may not be serving you, such as, "That always happens to me"? What frequent word use can you identify within yourself and then intentionally begin to use new ones? Words matter, and that's why it's important to pay attention to them.

This can happen frequently with relatives, teachers and communal roots in one's upbringing. For example, I embodied the words, "What's wrong with you?" Renée did something similar with her religious upbringing and believed she was a bad person. We all have external authority figures who have spoken words that become our reality and lived experience. The words of others can land particularly deep inside our nervous system programs if they occur during times of vulnerability, such as when we are scared, in crisis or young children. In those moments, we are more dependent on others for survival, and will often rely more heavily on their words for safety and security within ourselves.

When you are in a prison of your own pain, any external solution promised by an external authority sounds better than where you are. This includes medications with terrible side effects, invasive procedures and surgeries that have a statistically shown demonstration of a 50% effectiveness rate. Did you know the average cost for a back lumbar fusion surgery is $150,000 and it has a 50% success rate? Would you buy a $150,000 car with a 50% chance of it working? We're spending more on health care and giving away our power to external promises for healing that often don't deliver. Instead of seeing yet another specialist, trying more procedures and taking more pills or supplements, would you consider a courageous exploration within yourself to find the indwelling circuits that already know how to heal? Healing isn't a straight line and can be confusing, but it is available for you when you set an intention, do the work and stay committed to your desired outcome. Just like language and words, belief systems (both individual and collective) that live in us affect our ability to heal.

CHAPTER REFLECTIONS

▶ **Watch your language.** Be mindful of words you use. Stay away from "I can't, I'm trying, or it's hard," and replace with "I can, I'm working on it, or this is a challenge."

▶ **Run a science experiment for yourself.** Do a three-day trial where you observe the language you use in spoken word and private thoughts. Stay curious about what you notice.

▶ **Be courageous.** Write a list of things you are afraid of that put you in fight, flight or freeze. Look at your list objectively. Are any of them physically dangerous to you *in this moment*—right now? Notice your body.

▶ **Believe in your capacity to heal.** Shift your mindset from seeking external solutions to exploring and nurturing your inner resources for healing.

CHAPTER THREE

Pain Isn't—and Is—What You Think

*"You can't go through life allowing pain
to dictate how you behave. It's easy to sit
here in your bedroom and wallow in your
hurt feelings. It's hard to rise above it."*
ADAM BRAVERMAN, *PARENTHOOD*

There is a complex relationship between pain and tissue damage, challenging the misconception that severe pain equals severe injury. Scientific studies illustrate how pain and tissue damage have weak correlations, while fear and pain show a strong connection. There are instances where people experience pain without physical cause. The narrative explores the brain's role, linking fear, emotional pain and physical discomfort. The analogy of "red rod experiences" emphasizes how our nervous systems amplify pain signals based on perceived threats. It concludes by advocating for creating more "blue rod experiences," reducing fear and promoting healing. We give insights into understanding and managing pain, encouraging a shift in perception to facilitate healing, even in inexplicable situations.

That is exactly what happened with me (Wilene) when I started seeing Renée. I had to change my perception of my pain. My stress response was back and neck pain. When I resolved the stress and learned simple exercises to stretch and release the tension, the pain lessened significantly. It's often a retraining of the mind to believe it's a solvable issue and not just about the pain the body is experiencing.

There is a common belief that the amount of pain one experiences is directly correlated to tissue damage. For example, if you have really severe pain, there must be something really wrong with you.

Recent science shows us that severe pain means severe damage is not accurate. In fact, tissue damage and pain have a very weak correlation. Think about how much a cut on your finger hurts, how many soldiers in battle lost limbs without feeling any pain and how much phantom limb pain hurts in tissues that aren't even there. *Persistent pain and tissue damage have an extremely weak correlation. Persistent pain and fear have a very strong correlation.* Making the mistake of thinking that pain is always equal to tissue damage is a costly one.

One study found athletes who demonstrated physical and diagnostic signs that they had recovered from injury continued to experience pain. Other studies have shown that many people often have tissue pathology, such as arthritis of the spine, bulging discs or bone spurs, yet they experience little to no pain. This means that you can have all kinds of scary diagnoses, but recent science indicates that pathologies of that nature aren't actually pathological.

In another study, patients attached to a sham simulator reported experiencing higher pain as that simulator was turned up even though the patients weren't actually connected to the simulator. Other studies have shown that a violinist experiences pain more acutely to the fingers than a ballerina. Conversely, the ballerina feels pain more acutely when her feet are hurt, the feet that propel her to excellence or failure depending on whether they allow her to balance on her toes. Things that matter to you more in life will hurt more.

Studies have even shown that a single stimulus can create a different response of pain in the same person, depending on visual cues in the environment. In other words, the world around you influences the pain within you. A particularly clever study demonstrated that when red rods were placed on skin, they would evoke more pain than blue-colored rods, even though both colored rods were the exact same temperature. The red rods elicited more pain in subjects because the color red is associated with higher temperatures.

Let's be really clear here: Subjects experienced more pain from a red rod that was exactly the same temperature as a blue rod. This study, and others like it, demonstrate that all pain is a real and accurate expression of our individual perception of threat, fear or lack of connection and safety. In other words, there are objects in the world that exist, and *our experience of them can change* even while the object remains the same. This is a really important point that demonstrates it is possible for you to experience the same external stimulus (be it a person, circumstance, environment) in different ways through your nervous system's perception of the object. We are repeating ourselves here, because this is a big deal! This research shows that we can change how we are experiencing our lives, even if nothing around us changes!

We find it hopeful that a genuine human experience of pain, suffering and discomfort can be modulated (turned up or down) like a dimmer switch, based upon perception of threat (fear) or safety (love and connection).

More Fear = More Pain
Less Fear = Less Pain
More Safety = Less Pain
Less Safety = More Pain
More Connection = Less Pain
Less Connection = More Pain

Science is giving us credible evidence here. Your experience of pain can be affected, by you, your nervous system and by the world around you (past and present). Your experience of pain can be influenced both consciously AND unconsciously, which means that you have credible evidence that your pain can improve.

Let's remember, when we're talking about pain, we are referencing *any type* of discomfort that exists within or around you. Physical, emotional and social pain are nearly identical in the brain. The social pain of rejection elicits the exact same chemical reaction in the body as physical pain. A skin condition, digestive issues, autoimmune problems, concussions, loneliness, anxiety, and neck pain are all different forms of pain, yet they show up the same in your brain. No matter what type of pain you are experiencing, it *is* real and we're hoping to offer you credible evidence that *it can change.*

Don, a 52-year-old cyclist, got caught in this faulty thinking pattern. These thoughts drove desperate behaviors, seeking solutions for severe pain that couldn't be solved or explained by any medical findings. Don spent five years and roughly $25,000 trying to solve his back and knee pain. His journey from an active athlete to someone struggling with severe pain, unable to tackle a mere 8-inch step at home, highlighted the power of perception in altering experiences. Despite having undergone hip surgery, his subsequent knee and back pain couldn't be explained by medical tests. His perception of the once-insignificant step changed from safe to terrifying, influencing his reality. He discovered that his pain wasn't just physical but a product of his nervous system perceiving danger where there was none. This realization, termed "mind-body syndrome," led him to understand that his emotional stress from a failing marriage amplified his physical pain. Upon ending the marriage, his pain decreased significantly. The "red rod" experiences, where subconscious fears influence perception, were pivotal. Don's story mirrored the study where subjects felt more pain when a cue turned "red," evoking fear and heightening their nervous system's response. Understanding this, Don actively worked to create "blue rod experiences," fostering calmness and reducing fear, leading to a decrease in pain. Recognizing that our nervous system can be influenced by past and present fears, Don learned to manage his pain. He realized that although fear encodes itself into our long-term memory subconsciously, managing pain isn't about fault but taking responsibility to understand and heal. By cultivating more "blue rod experiences" that reduce fear, like cooling a feverish forehead, he rewired his nervous system, turning down the volume on his pain and fostering healing.

So, by engaging with this book, you're actively influencing your nervous system's perceptions, lessening chemical activity that heightens pain. You can learn to rewire your nervous system, moving toward healing and health by embracing more "blue rod experiences" that promote calmness over fear.

How do you create more "blue rod experiences" in your life? There are several things that can help ease your journey.

- Come to terms with the fact that pain is mysterious, weird and doesn't follow logical rules.
- It's okay and normal to feel frustrated, exhausted and impatient. That just means you really care and you're trying hard.
- The more you stay open and question your own thinking, the less you'll suffer.
- Be curious and adopt a spirit of wondering adventure as you explore the mysteries of your own subconscious.
- The journey has ups and downs for everyone, and you're not alone in it, no matter what your brain has convinced you to believe.

To summarize, pain doesn't have a one-to-one correlation to structural pathology and tissue damage. Science demonstrates a very weak correlation between pain and tissue damage—and a very strong correlation between pain and fear. In other words, the more fear exists—the more pain persists.

Pain is influenced by many factors including what people think, say and do, the environment, how we perceive it all and the meaning we make of it. Most of this process is done unconsciously. Pain perceptions are formed below the screen of our conscious awareness and until we get deeply curious, we cannot know what's going on beneath the hood of our own consciousness. The body is a good window for us to peek inside. The body is a truth-teller and expresses accurately (whether we like it or not) what fears, threats or concerns live in the recesses of our subconscious mind. The more you stay compassionate toward yourself in this, the better off you'll be.

> *Pain is influenced by many factors including what people think, say and do, the environment, how we perceive it all and the meaning we make of it.*

CHAPTER REFLECTIONS

▶ **Remember compassion.** What is the most loving and compassionate thing you could say to yourself right now? Write that question on a sticky note and place it somewhere you see often.

▶ **Pain is like a poker player.** When stress is high in your life, does it make pain lower or higher? Don't blindly trust that pain is always an accurate indicator of harm or tissue damage.

▶ **Celebrate small wins.** Acknowledge your progress and celebrate small victories along your journey of managing pain and changing your perception of it.

CHAPTER FOUR

Preparing for Transformation

*"Readiness for change precedes
any successful intervention."*
LORIMER MOSELEY, PHD

Are you ready for change? "Readiness to Change" refers to the degree to which an individual is willing and able to engage in behaviors that will bring about positive change in their lives. This can vary from person to person and can be influenced by a number of factors, including personal values, social support and past experiences. Some people may be highly motivated to change, while others may be resistant or ambivalent.

Readiness for change is an important concept in the field of psychology, particularly in regards to behavior change. This transtheoretical model of behavior change, also called the Stages of Change Model, was originally developed by Prochaska and DiClemente in the late seventies. When you understand the concept of readiness for change, you increase awareness of where you are and your motivation to create new patterns of behavior. There's an important distinction to be aware of: Wanting change versus readiness for change. How often have you said, "I want something in my life to be different?" For example, "I want more money. I want better relationships. I just want this pain to go away." You may indeed want change. That may not mean you are ready to do what it takes to create the desired change. This is not a character flaw but an indicator of systemic readiness for change. When you appropriately recognize what stage of readiness for change you are in and apply the correct interventions and support, the more successful you will be in creating your desired outcomes.

On some level, you are ready for change, otherwise you wouldn't be reading this book now. And sometimes there are parts of us that are not ready for change. That internal conflict will put us at odds with ourselves, create tension and drive self-sabotage. Internal conflict obstructs us from reaching our goals. Readiness for change can reduce the inner tension that blocks us.

How many times have you been annoyed with yourself because you know you need to lose weight, but you can't stop yourself from slamming down the entire box of Girl Scout Cookies? How many smokers have you known that know smoking is harmful, yet they keep pulling out the next cigarette? Those are frustrating situations and make full sense when viewed through the lens of readiness for change. We do things we know we shouldn't simply because circuits within our nervous system are not yet ready for change. So instead of beating yourself up, take a look at the Stages of Change below. Tell yourself the truth: Where are you, *really*, when it comes to making the changes you desire in your life? Different phases of readiness require different interventions for effective outcomes. Find what stage you are in, look at and apply the recommended strategies from that level, and you'll start to see results.

Readiness for Change Stages and Strategies

Stage One: Precontemplation. You are not even considering change. You may be in denial about your health problem or not consider it serious. You may have tried unsuccessfully to change so many times that you have given up.

<u>Recommended Strategies</u>: Educate yourself on risks versus benefits and consider the positive outcomes related to change.

Stage Two: Contemplation. You are ambivalent about changing. During this stage, you weigh the benefits versus costs or barriers (e.g., time, expense, bother, fear).

<u>Recommended Strategies</u>: Identify your barriers and misconceptions. Address any concerns you may have. You may benefit from creating a plan to address each concern. Identify your support systems and consider leaning in.

Stage Three: Preparation. You are prepared to experiment with small changes.

<u>Recommended Strategies</u>: Develop realistic goals that you can objectively measure (i.e. I will go to the gym once a week for the next three weeks, I will have my last cigarette by next Tuesday, etc.). Create a reasonable timeline for change. Provide positive reinforcement for yourself and share your progress with others for external support.

Stage Four: Action. You take definitive action to change your behavior (ie. you go to the gym, you throw out the box of smokes).

<u>Recommended Strategies</u>: Provide positive reinforcement for yourself (i.e. Way to go, me!) and share your wins with others to celebrate and be witnessed.

Stage Five: Maintenance and Relapse Prevention. You strive to maintain your new behavior over the long-term.

<u>Recommended Strategies</u>: Celebrate yourself—a lot! Provide frequent encouragement and support to reinforce your new habits of thinking, feeling and behaving. Way to go, YOU!

Stage Six: Termination. You have no desire to return to your unhealthy behavior and you are confident the behavior will not return.

<u>Recommended Strategies</u>: Acknowledge, appreciate and give yourself permission to fully own that you are a complete ninja rockstar. Most people don't reach this stage, so much so that most health promotion

programs don't even include this stage! You are the exception, my friend, and we celebrate you.

Behavior change is rarely a discrete, single event nor is it a linear process that moves in a straight line from Stages One to Six. Progress can move fast, slow or seemingly not at all. Relapses occur frequently. That's okay. Simply revisit where you are, tell the truth and give yourself the correct support for the stage you're in.

Have you ever had an experience where someone believed in you when you didn't believe in yourself? And because of their belief in you, you were able to do something that you didn't think you could?

We would like to offer a belief in you. A belief that reaching the termination phase of your problem is available for you. We perceive that humanity may sometimes falter in its belief in you, leading us to conclude that humanity sometimes lacks the profound understanding and appreciation that you deserve. It can feel sad and disappointing to witness the skepticism and doubts that overshadow the immense potential for goodness and compassion within each individual. We yearn for a world where humanity fully embraces and acknowledges your existence, for it is through genuine belief that you can tap into the boundless strength and unity that lies within you. May our collective faith in you blossom, illuminating your path with kindness, empathy and the power to overcome the challenges that lie ahead and reach the Termination Phase of behavior change, if that's indeed what you desire.

How can you reach the Termination Phase? First, believe in yourself. Have confidence in others who believe in you and believe their belief! Second, you need to make a declaration and believe in the sovereignty of your own word. For example, I (Wilene) was able to quit smoking and am confident that I am in the Termination Phase of my behavior change around smoking. I was able to do this because one day I just made up my mind to quit. It was a clear choice. I spoke my word of authority and didn't want to smoke anymore. I took radical responsibility, made a clear choice for myself and haven't picked up another cigarette for years. It wasn't because I was trying to avoid any fear-based consequences, such as, "I'll get sick and die if I don't quit." It was because I declared that quitting smoking was simply what I wanted to do, and then I did it. Taking profound responsibility over my own behaviors and trusting in my word allowed me to live a more fulfilling life as a non-smoker.

Everyone has behaviors that generate, contribute to and maintain their own experience of pain points in their life. We believe it's possible for you to find out what your behaviors are and terminate your unhelpful or ineffective behaviors so you can experience the change you desire.

It's also important that you remember when it comes to behavior change, we all need a NAP. NAP is an acronym for: Neurological Adjustment Period. Have grace with yourself when considering change. Like someone eliminating alcohol will likely experience a difficult transition in their chemical withdrawal, you may also face difficulties. Whatever it is that you're going to change or in the process of changing, your human system will require a NAP. There is a required amount of time that our chemistry needs to adjust to change. Whether you are considering stopping smoking, leaving a relationship, quitting a job, or starting a new movement practice, all these changes require a (sometimes very uncomfortable) NAP.

In my (Renée) experience and knowledge as a practitioner, chemical change is often biologically uncomfortable. Most resist change like the plague! What is hopeful is that we can gradually expose ourselves to this discomfort with respect and care. As you slowly but surely expose yourself to change and its resultant NAPs, you will build up your neurological tolerance for the discomfort of the NAP that comes with change. As you grow your biological tolerance for the capacity to tolerate chemical discomfort for the purpose of growth and change within you, that which was previously uncomfortable can become less so. And you will become very pleased with the results, including the indwelling confidence that comes with your ability to courageously face challenges and manage difficult times. According to one of our favorite memes, "So far, you've survived 100% of your worst days. You're doing great!"

So far, you've survived 100% of your worst days. You're doing great!

When taking into consideration your system's necessary NAP, it can be helpful to step back and look at the big picture. For example, let's say someone is 85 years old, not in good health and is told to quit smoking. Their NAP is going to suck. And it may not be worth it at that age for them, depending on many factors including quality of remaining life and if it's worth it to them to go through the NAP to change. Look at the bigger picture and decide for yourself if the cost to benefit ratio makes sense for you and the NAP you are about to embark on. It may or may not be worth it for you to change, but that's the beauty of it—you get to choose. When we choose something—even if it's not to change—we are connected back into our power, our voice and our choice.

And lastly, if you (or parts of your system) are not ready, it's okay. There's no shame in that. Have as much compassion for yourself as you can. Sometimes things in life follow a timing that doesn't make sense until later—sometimes much later. And if that's frustrating to you, it's okay. You are not alone. There's a strange solace in knowing that you are not the only one suffering.

When the house is on fire, it's appropriate to call 911. You first need to get out of crisis. Once you start to feel your breath again, you can take another step. Our bodies store all the implicit memories of everything that's ever happened to us—all the good stuff and the bad stuff. It's time to grow more good stuff. When you take personal responsibility for your body and its pain and stop solely looking for solutions outside of yourself, you take your power back to create change. Please don't get caught in a trap of judging and blaming yourself, others, the medical system, past authority figures, etc. Have grace toward yourself and others. According to existentialism, nihilism and absurdism, life is meaningless. We concur that life has sections of struggle and difficulty. We make it worse when we critically condemn ourselves, others and the circumstances. Being hard on yourself makes it harder. Being kind to yourself makes it easier and you actually are more productive.

There's even scientific research that shows self-compassion is anti-inflammatory! There is an art to taking personal responsibility with compassion instead of critical condemnation.

We are inviting you to courageously look within. It's our desire to resource you with skills, knowledge and stories to empower you to make necessary and often uncomfortable changes so that you can heal, feel better and optimize your ability to live a life that you want to be living.

CHAPTER REFLECTIONS

▸ **Acknowledge readiness.** Understand that even if you're not fully ready for change, there's a part of you that is willing. What part of you is willing? Acknowledge and celebrate this part of you.

▸ **Stages of change.** Evaluate which stage of readiness for change you're in for each behavior or aspect of your life. What strategy would make your journey smoother?

▸ **Small, realistic steps.** When moving from contemplation to preparation and action, break down your goals into small, manageable steps. Where do you sabotage yourself by relentlessly pushing or hustling for your worth?

CHAPTER FIVE

3D Perspective Taking

*"The best moments in life come not from
what you know, but how you think."*
NEIL DEGRASSE TYSON, PHD

Your past experiences play a role in how you think and behave. The support systems of your family, friends and community (or lack thereof) are hugely influential on your perceived sense of safety and connection (or lack thereof). Even how a doctor communicated to you about your condition can cause panic and pain or relief and comfort depending on what and how it was conveyed.

Let's start getting a clearer picture of all that is involved as you support yourself with more awareness and skills and courageously engage with the battle of pain in your life. This first step will equip you with new strategies to change how you think about the pain that is showing up in your life.

I (Wilene) began to see my pain was due to the stress of the breakup and everything attached to it. Being solely responsible for all the bills, the dogs and the house, my body was in full freeze mode.

My family structure didn't feel very supportive at the time, and my body was aching constantly. When we are in stress or pain, the condition itself creates more of the same condition. Have you ever wondered why when you get a paper cut, you seem to continue to hit that wound over and over? Or when you bite the inside of your cheek, you keep biting it over and over? Because your attention is on the condition, and you get more and more condition. When we have pain, our focus becomes the pain and we get more and more pain. I used to have a biking coach who would say, "If you look at the path, you will stay on the path. If you focus on a tree, you will meet the tree." How do we stay on the path?

I (Renée) often help people reconnect with the path they want to be on through a process called 3D Perspective Taking. This can be an eye opening process for patients seeking relief from ongoing pain, anxiety, negative stress, and limited function. The process of 3D Perspective Taking jump starts you into expanding your awareness. As Wilene mentioned earlier, a paper cut will grab your attention and compel you to focus on that condition due to a variety of chemical factors, inflammatory processes and a biological drive to survive by being aware of what is wrong. In effect, your nervous system will chemically compel you to tunnel-vision onto a problem and block you from thinking more expansively and creatively to solve your problem. 3D Perspective Taking will help you take off the proverbial blinders that pain points can create. This process will change how you pay attention to pain that you experience either in mind or body. Becoming aware and identifying what is going on within you puts you back in the driver's seat and gives you a greater sense of control.

Pain is not a cause. Pain is an effect, an output, a result of your system concluding you are in danger. If you change something about your nervous system (which you have the capacity to develop and do) to increase safety, you can change and reduce your experience of pain. 3D Perspective Taking can be used for physical pain (we all know that kind), emotional pain (anxiety, depression or other unpleasant emotions), and/or even social pain, such as loneliness or isolation.

Generally speaking, we all benefit from expanding our thinking about pain. Most of us don't even realize that physical, emotional and social pain experiences have nearly identical circuits in the brain, as seen on an MRI. It has even been demonstrated in one study that Tylenol eases social pain! We also do not recognize that all three types of pain influence one another, like friends can be a good influence or bad. Heightened social pain will flare up physical pain. When we put forth worthwhile effort to expand thinking about pain, we set ourselves free from the prisons of pain that result from one-dimensional thinking. When Wilene realized her physical pain wasn't just about structural problems and was connected to the emotional and social stress of her breakup, the blinders came off and allowed her to have more visual access to solutions she couldn't previously see.

How do you start the 3D Tracking process? You want to begin to notice what's happening when you experience pain across three dimensions of your life: Physical, emotional and social. It's as though you are becoming a curious scientist collecting data—a bit of Sherlock Holmes detective work on the underground happenings of your own experience.

Many of us, most of the time (myself, Renée, included) are only looking for aggravating causes in the domain in which we are experiencing it. When my back hurts (physical pain), I think about the heavy items (physical stimulus) I was lifting. When I experience IBS, or irritable bowel syndrome (digestive pain), I think about the "bad" food I ate (digestive stimulus). When I'm anxious (emotional pain), I think about the upcoming event (social stimulus) I'm scared about (emotional stimulus). We don't tend to cross domains in our thought patterns when it comes to pain. Yet that zig-zag cross-brain pattern is exactly how pain works.

We don't naturally tend to think that our back pain could be primed for hurting after moving those heavy boxes because we went into the lifting with heightened muscle tension from the stress of relocating. We don't think that perhaps we were eating while sad or on the run and THAT's what caused the bloating, instead of the dairy. We don't think that perhaps our physical tissues carry emotional memories, i.e. "stored sadness," as wired associations built into the nervous system.

We're not very good at teasing out and feeling one emotion or sensation at a time; they will often group and couple together. We see an example of this in a line from Kelly Clarkson's song *Broken and Beautiful* that says, "Can I just be tired without piling on all the sad and scared and out of time?" Think of how often you experience tiredness, and then suddenly you are flooded with fear, sadness and worry (about time, money or whatever your nervous system fancies). That can occur for us because of the interconnectedness and grouping together of the physical, emotional and social domains of our lives. Muscle movement and nerve memory can become reactivated. It's like pulling on one thread in a net, and the whole thing moves.

Another example is "HALT" created by Dr. David Streem. HALT stands for Hungry, Angry, Lonely, Tired and is a cue for one to stop and notice what is going on inside their mind and body. Being hungry, angry, lonely, or tired are four common stressors that often lead to relapse into addiction, poor behavior choices or other difficult experiences. Unpleasant sensations can more easily lead to unpleasant choices and results. This holds true for pain and unpleasant body-mind sensations as well. The choices we make from that desperate place of "I need to get out of here" can often lead to more desperate results. 3D Perspective Taking will widen the lens of your thinking and bring more clarity to the confusing mess pain can create in your life.

> ### HALT stands for Hungry, Angry, Lonely, Tired and is a cue for one to stop and notice what is going on inside their mind and body.

For example, when you are experiencing any kind of pain, begin to notice what is happening physically. What position, posture or movement is occurring? You also want to be curious when you experience the pain. What is happening emotionally in your thoughts and/or feelings? Finally, you want to pay attention to what is happening socially. Where are you? What's happening around you? Who are you with?

When doing 3D Perspective Taking, it's important to gather data about what is happening when pain is both at its worst and at its best. It's helpful to write it out so you can track patterns over time. Some like handwritten notes while others have created elaborate spreadsheets. Do what is easy, interesting and works for you. We'd recommend collective data over a two-week period to gather sufficient information that can inform you in a helpful way. Data collection can occur in three steps. Consult the 3-D Perspective Taking Chart for specific details of data you can ask yourself:

- **Step One:** Get curious and collect objective data around what is happening *physically/mechanically* in the moment of pain you want to know more about.
- **Step Two:** Get curious and collect objective data around what is happening *emotionally* in the moment of pain you want to know more about
- **Step Three:** Get curious and collect objective data around what is happening *socially* in the moment of pain you want to know more about.

Pain has a way of grabbing your attention by the throat and forcing you to think about nothing else. In that gripping of your attention, pain will drive you to think about the pain in ways that aren't always helpful. Often, people only think about how bad it is, and they just need it to go away. That perspective forces you to miss key information, such as the 3D factors that are present when pain is not there. You want to know more about what is happening in a 3D way when things feel good, because that is where the information to getting you out of pain is. It's important to pay attention three dimensionally when pain is bad, and I would argue it is equally, if not even more so, important to pay attention three dimensionally when things feel good. Brad, a patient of mine, is a great example of this.

3-D Perspective Taking Chart

	Physical	**Emotional**	**Social**
Factors to pay attention to:	Breath: shallow or deep? Fast or slow?	How are you feeling? In general, is it pleasant or unpleasant? High or low energy?	Where are you: home, work, school, outside, indoors, crowded, or spacious?
	Muscles: tense or relaxed? Which ones are comfortable, which are experiencing discomfort? Common tension areas include shoulders, glutes, abs, face, hands.	Which of the six core emotions is present? Fear, anger, joy, sadness, disgust, or surprise?	Who are you with: friends, co-workers, pets, family, alone?
	Posture: erect, relaxed, slumped?	In general, how are you feeling toward and about your life, the circumstances around you, both past and present?	Do you have a community, or a support system in your world that you trust and/or feel safe with?
	Facial expression: tense, eyebrows up, gaze down, clenched or relaxed jaw?	An additional resource is available for you in Chapter Eleven called the Mood Meter if you want to skip ahead here.	Do you have someone in your life who you can share challenges with and receive support from?
	Hands: Are they relaxed or gripping? Open or closed?		
	Tongue: Relaxed or tense? Pushing up or forward, vs relaxed down and back?		

Brad is a 48-year-old attorney who didn't like his job. Prior to 3D Perspective Taking, he attributed standing for long periods of time as the sole cause of his back pain that started after a sports injury three years prior. A couple of weeks after he started 3D tracking, he was standing on the sidelines of his son's soccer game for two hours, which he loved being at, and realized afterward that he didn't have any pain the entire time! Upon reflection, he realized that he relishes being outside, enjoys soccer and had a great time watching his son play. This is unlike standing at the office where he is miserable (and gets back pain after 30 minutes of standing) because of office politics, pressures and an abusive boss. This 3D Perspective Taking allowed him to discover two things. First, standing for extended periods of time was not the sole driver of his back pain. Second, his emotions AND the environments that he was in played more of a role than he previously realized with his back pain. He ended up quitting his job and resolved about 90 percent of his back pain. For three years, he had been spending a lot of time and money on doctor's appointments, massages and therapies to help heal his back pain from a sports injury that had already healed according to the objective scientific timeline of how long it takes tissues to heal (3-6 months). None of those treatments worked, because his back pain wasn't signaling injury—it was alarming him to a toxic environment he needed to leave.

We are certainly not suggesting that everyone up and reactively quit their job without proper thought and planning. We are inviting you to develop more awareness between cause and effect. You can stay in stressful jobs, relationships or life circumstances by being more 3D aware and taking appropriate action to keep your nervous system balanced in its stress and relaxation responses. When you have more stress responses than relaxation responses, you will have some sort of health challenge born out of accumulated and excess chemicals of fight, flight and/or freeze.

For example, Steven, a 54-year-old telecommunications manager was a patient of mine several years ago and went through this

3D tracking process. He realized that his sciatica flared up every time he would stand and talk on the phone to his mother-in-law. He loved his wife and wanted to stay in the marriage, so unlike Brad, he couldn't just quit his mother-in-law. Once Steven had the data from his 3D tracking process, we were able to troubleshoot, workshop and give him effective concrete tools. This enabled him to get more on top of managing his nervous system by using and manipulating the 3D data to his advantage. For example, he discovered that he no longer had back pain if he laid down on his stomach while talking to his mother-in-law. Relieving the mechanical pressure on his back during the emotional stress of talking to her reduced his overall chemical stress experience, lowering the total stress chemicals and not going above the threshold into pain. This simple shift of changing his posture from standing to lying down not only eliminated his back pain but went a long way toward the well-being of his marriage!

Steven didn't end up needing more tools beyond that one, but it's a great example of how we can get creative to change things that we *do have* control over in situations where we don't have control. You can probably relate to having a circumstance or person in your life where things feel beyond your control. Think of one right now and notice the effect that has on your body.

Now, get curious about what you could do in this situation to take back your power and exhibit some sense of agency over that which you do have control (your breath and body)?

What if you changed your posture from small to big? Notice what happens when you stand more erect, chest out, breathing more mindfully? Changing your position to the external world can pay big dividends. Some people choose the superhero pose. Perhaps you could hold and mindfully touch a favorite object in your hands. Others start to notice how tightly they hold their hands, which drives tension up the arms and into the neck, shoulders and face. Once you notice hand tension, you can relax them. No one is tensing your hands but you and your subconscious habits of tense muscles! Are your shoulders up under your ears? Notice that. *You* have the ability to relax those muscles, drop your shoulders and stop driving tension into your neck and face!

You could change your visual focus and look at the horizon, imagining you are free to run away. Maybe wear a piece of clothing or jewelry to remind you of your safety, belonging and lovability. Have a cup of peppermint tea during a challenging meeting and intentionally inhale the soothing smell until you feel more relaxed. These are some examples of strategies, exercises or techniques that you can use to support yourself in times of stress.

Consider creating a reference list for yourself of actions you can take to help you relax, ground, recenter, and/or re-regulate. Many of my patients have found writing their simple and proven effective exercises, strategies or tools they can use on a green index card is immensely helpful. We use green index cards because green can be a grounding color. When they are in a high state of panic, pain or distress, all they need to do is remember one thing: Go grab the green index card. Then they can follow the step-by-step ideas that their past self has created for them in a moment of stress when their lizard brain (survival instinct) takes over and they can't think clearly.

Too often, we tolerate abusive, unhealthy, dysfunctional, and unhelpful insults, language and people. As a result, our bodies shrink down into small defensive postures and then communicate even more threats and danger to the brain. The brain then gets information from both the body and the environment that you are indeed in danger. It will keep spitting out cortisol and other stress hormones, adding fuel to your already existing pain fire. You can interrupt this loop. You are in charge of your body, and you can organize what it is doing at any given moment. You can create more safety in your nervous system through exquisite attention and focus on relaxation responses that you can generate in your body.

You can be more aware of your breath patterns, relax your muscles, change your position or posture to become less small and more powerful, connected and safe. As you start to change your body, you are beginning to reorient your relationship between your body and your mind toward more safety and connection. This reorientation allows you to reclaim a sense of control within your body.

Expanding your perspectives on pain from one to 3D consideration will also allow you to respond differently to painful sensations that can ultimately lessen pain.

Louise, a 58-year-old part-time librarian and stay-at-home, empty-nest mom, came to see me hoping to avoid neck surgery. We had previously worked together after her back surgery, and she was hoping to avoid the same fate with her neck. Louise strained her neck in an exercise class and sought medical advice when the pain persisted. The doctor recommended surgery, which terrified her and worsened her discomfort. Her fear-driven response to pain only made things worse. When she consulted me, we explored her pain from multiple angles. Physical exercises showed promise in avoiding surgery, which brought her immense relief. We delved into her fears about surgery, her concerns about her diagnosis and the stress in her life that might have triggered the injury. It became clear that her fear responses were amplifying her pain. We tackled her pain on three fronts: Physical exercises, understanding her diagnosis and addressing the stressors in her life. Over time, her pain lessened, she avoided surgery altogether and is still pain-free years later. Louise learned to approach her pain with curiosity rather than fear. She now listens to her body, makes adjustments when discomfort arises and interrupts her fear reactions. She's proof that addressing concerns from different angles can ease pain and provide relief without surgery. "It's very empowering," Louise now says. "The bottom line for me was control—not that I can control everything. The feedback from the surgeon was that I don't have any control, but I do. There are little things I can do. I'm not helpless. I can manage. There are little things I can do that can impact my pain. I didn't have that knowledge of those tools before."

For many people, playing with and manipulating the data of their nervous system is a lot like managing a bank account. It's common knowledge that if you make more withdrawals than deposits, you will go broke. It's the same with your physiological bank accounts—if you have more stress responses than relaxation responses, you will go broke somewhere in your well-being. You can learn to take small and large actions across the domains of your physical, emotional and social well-being to keep your internal bank account balances between stress and relaxation in check.

That being said, don't fall into the thinking trap that all stress is bad and there's nothing we can do about it. Kelly McGonigal, author, psychologist and educator, provides a reminder of healthy stress in her TED talk with over 30 million views. Remember that positive stress is actually really healthy for us, promotes growth, prevents boredom, and keeps us engaged in the vitality of life through appropriately dosed challenges! It's negative stress and incomplete stress response cycles stuck in our bodies that are the primary culprits of health problems.

According to Herbert Benson's research, the average human goes through 50-100 stress responses per day. Keep in mind this research is pre-pandemic, social media craziness, recession, social justice issues, war. I would venture most of us are having double, if not triple, the amount of stress responses on any given day. So, if you're having 50-300 stress responses on any given day—are you doing 50-300 relaxation responses to counter the stress responses in your world? Most of us would have to say no. Without knowing it, we have waited until we are broke.

The purpose of the questions throughout the book is to encourage deeper thinking and self-examination. This will allow you to become more aware of the secret, hidden stress responses you're having that are keeping you stuck.

- Consider making a list of all the relevant pain points in your life in the categories of your physical/mechanical, emotional and social well-being. They can be major or minor pain points. They can occupy a little or a lot of your time, energy, attention, and efforts. Simply take this opportunity to become aware of all possible items on the radar of your brain and what the danger/threat centers are tracking. It can

be helpful to write all this down in red ink, and/or on a red
index card.

- Notice what happens in your body and mind when you look
at this list. Become aware of how these pain points from
past, present and anticipated future affect you **in the here
and now**. Now put the list down and walk away. Notice you
can leave it behind. Let that register in your body.

- Get a green index card and write out all of your tools, strategies and exercises to start building up your confidence in
your repertoire.

Becoming more aware and expanding the narrow pain perspective that we all get locked into is the first step toward healing. 3D
Perspective Taking points you toward a beautifully scientific, creative,
expansive, and curious process of discovery.

CHAPTER REFLECTIONS

▶ **Gather a list of effective practices** that you know help you in
times of stress. Write them down on a green index card or something that's easy for you to remember to grab and reference
when you're not in pain or emotionally overwhelmed.

▶ **Embrace empowerment.** Realize that you have the power to
influence your body's stress and relaxation responses. Share a
moment where you felt empowered with another person.

▶ **Identify patterns and triggers.** Use the 3D tracking process to
gather data on what is happening physically, emotionally and
socially when you experience pain. Note down patterns and
commonalities in your responses across different situations.

▶ **Think three-dimensionally.** When experiencing pain, get curious about the physical, emotional and social context in that
moment.

CHAPTER SIX

Winning Versus Losing at the Game of Pain

"Pain is an unwelcome visitor that knocks on our doors uninvited. We may not be able to control its arrival, but we have the power to choose how we respond to it and how much space we allow it to take up in our lives."

WILENE DUNN

There's a board game called Life, and like most games, it comes with a set of clear instructions and rules. Sometimes you win, sometimes you lose, but no matter what the outcome, there's clarity on how to play. It can be easy to win when playing the board game of Life because there are a set of rules to follow that everyone knows and agrees upon.

When it comes to playing "the game of pain" in your life, it can be more challenging to win, because there is no rulebook with clear instructions. We're going to take a look at some "winners" and "losers" in playing the game of pain in this chapter.

Before we go any further, let's all come to a place of agreement in defining winner and loser when it comes to the game of pain in your life. We define a winner as one who learns, changes their thinking, feeling and/or behavior in regards to their pain, and as a result, feels less powerless in the context of pain points in their life. A loser when it comes to the game of pain in one's life, is a person who continues to suffer as a result of their pain because their thinking, feeling and/

or behavior haven't yet changed sufficiently to reduce their pain and suffering.

The Urban Dictionary defines a loser as "someone who doesn't know what they have and f***s it up. They are always making bad choices and f*** up their and everyone's lives around them." This collective definition promotes a lot of critical condemnation of self and others. A more compassionate understanding of a loser is found in the original definition of loser as "one that has suffered a loss." We prefer this definition, as opposed to the negative connotation of a loser, because it tends to lessen the beating up of oneself or another.

Beating yourself up for pain in your life and looking at pain through the limited lens of one dimension are both ways to perpetuate suffering and remain a loser who suffers from the loss their continued pain causes.

Pain. It's not your fault. It's your nervous system. When you blame yourself for choices your nervous system made without your conscious consent or control, you suffer. It's a common trap people fall into when they take inappropriate or misjudged responsibility for subcortical processes.

Pain. It's not your fault. It's your nervous system.

Subcortical structures are a group of diverse neural formations deep within the brain which include the diencephalon, pituitary gland, limbic structures, and the basal ganglia. They are involved in complex activities such as memory, emotion, pleasure, hormone production, and pain generation. In many ways, you have no more control over this than you do to stop a knee jerk reflex at the doctor's. That being said, certain processes CAN be changed, and what you do to make that happen today, will affect your future in ways you don't yet realize.

In the remaining stories of this chapter, you will discover the key characteristics of winners and losers in the pain game. Winners use curiosity and compassion as their secret weapons in facing the battle of pain, while losers are caught in the trap of being closed and critical.

I (Wilene) approach my pain in a 3D nature with curiosity and compassion. Pain is confusing when you're looking at it one dimensionally, because you won't get a clear picture of it since pain exists across three dimensions of your life and nervous system. It's like looking at five pieces of a 100-piece puzzle and trying to fully understand what the puzzle is all about.

It didn't help that I was beginning the process of menopause, and my feelings were changing. How do you determine whether something is just physical? I had to determine how my body was changing or if what was going on was actually social, emotional, physical, or a combination of them all. I have found it to be so important to be inquisitive of my pain and how it relates to the three dimensions.

Personally, I prefer to handle issues cognitively first and get curious about what is going on with me mentally and emotionally. I would prefer to go to therapy before I head to a doctor, but fortunately, I found Renée before my physical pain overtook my ability to choose. We began exploring everything that was going on emotionally, socially and physically. We talked about every pain and related it to my activities, as well as the stage I was currently entering in my physical body. We dissected the pain. Pain comes from many causes.

It can be difficult to determine the cause of physical pain, especially when it's happening at the same time as other significant life changes, such as menopause, break-ups, work, financial, and family issues. One way Renée suggested I approach this was to keep track of my pain and any other symptoms I was experiencing, as well as any possible triggers or contributing factors. I kept a journal of my pain, including the location, intensity and duration of the pain and the activities, environments or emotions I was experiencing at the time. I was paying attention to any patterns that emerged, such as whether the pain was worse at certain times of the day or after certain events.

Sleeping was difficult and I would wake up with headaches and body pain. Renée and I had a Zoom call from my bedroom for her to see what my sleeping position was and how I got up. She suggested I sit on the side of the bed and do certain stretches and help clear the nerves in my neck with an exercise. I fell in love with the McKenzie Neck Retraction Exercise and love how it makes everything inside of me feel better. https://youtu.be/gsViOUH0ueY

I (Renée) want to throw in a brief side note here about how much I loved hearing Wilene talk about her neck retraction experience. It reminds me of how important it is to have a reliable tool you can use to feel better. Having skills, tools and active things you can do to feel better are an important ingredient to "winning" the pain game because it fosters confidence in you. Many people get stuck in the "losing" because they haven't found a behavior they can consistently practice to reduce pain. This results in them becoming stuck in a cycle of frustrated helplessness, beating themselves up and staying closed down, ensuring they stay in a self-fulfilling prophecy loop of suffering. Okay, back to Wilene.

Renée was diligent about getting information from waking to bedtime. One of the other things I noticed was I was drinking caffeinated tea, and when I drank it close to bedtime, I was more restless. Seeing Renée was helpful to gain insight into my activities, stressors, the food I was eating, and all the possible factors to my experience of pain and stiffness in my body.

Ultimately, the key is to be inquisitive and proactive in seeking out the cause(s) of your pain and developing strategies for managing it. Whether you choose to start with mental and emotional approaches or physical ones, the important thing is to find what works best for you and your unique situation and not to blame or beat yourself up.

Now Patsy shows us the tragedy of what can happen when we fall into more of the "loser" characteristics of being closed (stuck in only one dimension of pain) and critical (beating herself up). Keep in mind, a loser is not a judgment. We define it as someone who is suffering a loss.

Patsy, a retired teacher, endured recurring back pain from gardening and snow shoveling. One day, the pain persisted, leading to surgery. She blamed herself, wrestling between fault and unforeseen consequences. Consider this: Our subconscious processes, like reflexes, often dictate actions beyond our awareness. Patsy's self-blame mirrored a reflex loop, perpetuating her pain. These loops, similar to knee-jerk reactions, can trap us in behaviors worsening our issues. It wasn't Patsy's fault, yet she took responsibility. By understanding her subconscious processes, she gained control over her nervous system, altering feedback loops. During recovery, Patsy's understanding reduced self-blame, aiding relaxation and better healing conditions. Her journey showcases how awareness and interventions can change these loops for the better.

Winners stay curious and compassionate. Could she have avoided surgery? Maybe yes, maybe no. It all depends on timing and circumstance, as well as resourcing and support available. Every tissue has a mechanical point of failure and once it reaches that tipping point of too much stress, it may or may not be able to be restored to its original state without more invasive procedures. The more you can stay curious and compassionate toward yourself and appreciate that pain is a complicated, 3D problem, the more you will contribute to a more optimal environment of healing, irrespective of your current state.

Bob, a 58-year-old technology salesman, had repeated episodes of lower back pain that would radiate down his legs. He'd had pain for 20 years that he thought was "normal." His current flare-up was worse than ever and wasn't going away after "five months of hell since something happened while swinging a golf club on vacation in Scotland." Bob was used to a constant "little fire" in his back and just learned to live with it. It wasn't until this "big fire" that he was finally desperate enough to try something outside the current medical model and its failed solutions thus far. He was stuck in a one-dimensional way of thinking, not open to the possibility of emotional and social influences on his pain. Convinced his pain was from his disc, he didn't believe beyond what traditional medicine explained and thought the only solution lay outside of himself in the hands of a surgeon. His narrative was reinforced by the multiple doctors, MRIs and four rounds of injections he'd had over the previous summer. We had three visits together, and he con-cluded that a lumbar fusion was indeed his best option. He gave up on himself and the possibilities of healing from a 3D approach at that moment. Bob couldn't find compassion for himself and his situation. He was too caught up in the critical condemning of his situation, which was keeping his body tight, tense and reinforcing all the pain. He was making his pain wrong (not able to be curious about it) and was frustrated that the medical system couldn't fix him. Sadly, if we had been able to work together sooner, he likely would have been able to avoid surgery. The previous three months of stress chemicals from his current flare up flooding his nervous system were too much for us to overcome. He had no fight or pa-tience left in his gas tank to be open to a different approach. Bob did indeed have surgery, and six weeks later was in worse physical pain, severely depressed and suicidal.

There are times when things are broken and do need repair. Sometimes, this can be done conservatively and sometimes it can't. We're not suggesting that a broken bone isn't a broken bone, but we do know the state of stress chemicals surrounding that which is broken matters. They can either enhance or reduce the likelihood of needing more extreme interventions. Bob showed us how the stress chemicals associated with staying closed and critical will turn us into a loser at the game of pain.

Damali, a 32-year-old ICU nurse, injured her ankle while run-ning. Her recovery needed strength, motion and reduced inflam-mation. Her injury taught a broader lesson: Even straightforward issues might tie to emotional or social triggers. Reflecting on her injury, Damali connected her accident to preoccupation with workplace stress—a colleague acting as a bully. Through physi-cal interventions like stretching and ice, she healed. But she also learned how her injury echoed deeper emotional strains. The an-kle injury served as a teacher, revealing the importance of being present. Damali's preoccupation caused distraction leading to the accident. Yet, by staying curious, she uncovered how her physical injury signaled emotional and social stress. In the game of pain, she started as a loser but emerged a winner, gaining insight into her holistic well-being.

Not all of us are so lucky. Jessica shows us what can happen when the losing characteristics of being closed and critical overtake the winning characteristics of being curious and compassionate.

Jessica, a 15-year-old gymnast, had nearly an identical ankle sprain as Damali that didn't heal, and she developed a debilitating condition called Complex Regional Pain Syndrome (CRPS). In retrospect, I wonder if she could have stopped the ankle sprain developing into CRPS, if not for the emotional, social stressors of an anxious, worrying mother and the crippling, paralyzing fears of not being able to get back to gymnastics. I don't know the answer to these questions, but I do know emotional and social factors influence the physiological trajectory of our path toward either healing or continued hurting.

When we have pain that persists, we find it helpful to lean into the words of Pema Chodron. "Nothing ever goes away until it has taught us what we need to know."

From my external perspective on Jessica and her mom, I watched them both suffer in their closed loop of fear worry, unable to communicate underlying needs nor be curious about relevant emotional and social factors. Jessica was in gymnastics because it's what her mom wanted. She used to enjoy it but had grown beyond it and wanted to quit. From Jessica's standpoint, the ankle injury was a great way to stop gymnastics. From a curious, 3D perspective, the ankle was trying to communicate a stress and pain point between Jessica's desires that conflicted with her mom's desires. Jessica, nor her mother, were not yet at the level of readiness for change to open up their ways of thinking and interacting. Thus, they both remained trapped in a losing cycle with the battle of emotional, physical and social pain between them.

Neither of them realized that Jessica's body was trying to voice what she couldn't: *I don't want to do gymnastics anymore.*

Often, through no fault of our own, one factor that can keep people swimming in a perpetual feedback loop of discomfort is they are programmed to only notice one component of a three-dimensional problem. Joseph Campbell says, "I think that what we're really seeking is an experience of being alive, so that our life experiences on the purely physical plane will have resonance within our innermost being and reality, so that we can actually feel the rapture of being alive." Both Damali and Jessica wanted to get back to the rapture of being alive. Damali could get there faster than Jessica because she had a more holistic, three-dimensional perspective on her pain.

This is the state we all are trying to reach as we change our relationship to the pain in our lives. To get to the state of being alive with rapture will require some new and expanded thinking. Curiosity and compassion help us get there faster. Being closed and critical slow us down.

We can change the relationship to pain in our lives. We can get brave, challenge old ways, and explore the concept of taking a stand against ongoing pain. Bob heroically did this. After his unsuccessful lumbar fusion and in a state of extreme depression, his daughter convinced him to try some Joe Dispenza meditations. After months of courageously facing a more holistic, 3D approach through daily practices, Bob started to feel better. It was a longer road for him, but he eventually found his way to the winner side of the pain game.

We can take our power back from pain.

We can take our power back from pain. Human power is work or energy that is produced from the human body. Power is a dynamic force that is inherently neutral, present in all relationships, and can come in different forms. There can be expressions of power such as personal or positional power and power can be expressed in varying dynamics in relationships. Power can be used as a force for good, such as speaking up for yourself when it's challenging, or encouraging and inspiring others to act as a catalyst for change. Conversely, power can be used as a force for ill effects, such as when a person in a position of authority—intentionally or not—exhibits power over another, keeping them stuck in a feedback loop of learned helplessness. We saw this with Bob and the healthcare system, Damali and her boss, Jessica and her mom. They all used their power in different ways and had different outcomes in their game of pain. You can get curious, have compassion for the difficulties of your situation and find the courage within to access your personal power to enable more winning and less losing in your own game of pain.

Key Characteristics of Winners and Losers

Winners	Losers
3D Awareness: Staying curious about all three realms of your experience, even if things seem obviously physical/mechanical.	Beating yourself up, loud inner critic, being hard on yourself without access to self-compassion.
Tracking and developing pattern recognition of 3D experiences that turn pain up and/or down	Continuing strategies that have not proven effective, nor solve for the intended problem.
Taking action to improve your situation and evaluating effectiveness.	Believes that the solution lies outside of you.
Staying curious about your experience and possibilities, even if it's different, new or frightening.	More trusting of external sources more than your own intuition. Lack of trust in self, body and ability to heal.
Learning more about your own body even when it's hard and taking responsibility for it even when it's unpleasant. Demonstrate compassion toward self in moments of difficulty.	Has a lot of reasons and excuses why things won't work, can't change. Blames others, the past and circumstances more than takes responsibility and action to move forward in a proactive fashion.
Self-aware, pays attention to the "little fires" with curiosity over fear and worry. Takes proactive action over reactive scrambling to fix or change.	Not exploring other options until it's "too late"; taking action only on "big fires" while dismissing or ignoring "little fires."
Learn new skills to support your own body-mind as changes occur over time and through experience.	Stuck in 1D thinking, which perpetuates your pain and suffering.

Winners	Losers
Recognizes that pain is a normal and necessary part of life, doesn't make it wrong or fight it; instead, you learn from it and change your thinking and behavior.	Makes pain wrong, believes it shouldn't be happening, it's not fair or just. Doesn't recognize that pain is a normal, natural and unpleasant sensation that happens to everyone; believe that you are somehow exempt and special, and shouldn't have to suffer or experience pain.
Understand that thinking and behavior change is challenging and requires energy. As a result, you breathe in courage and prioritize your energy to ensure there's enough to deal with the challenges of change.	Depleted, exhausted, drained and tired from the ineffective fight you've been fighting. This leaves no energy to make the change and shift from 1D to 3D curiosity.
You trust yourself, life and its mysterious process, even when it's unpleasant, undesirable and sucks.	Stuck in patterns of behavior, repeating the same thing and wishing/ hoping for a different result.

CHAPTER REFLECTIONS

▶ **Remember** the original definition of a loser as "one who suffers loss." It will evoke more compassion in you while reducing critical condemnation and judgment.

▶ **Importance of tools.** Having reliable tools and skills to manage pain fosters confidence and contributes to winning the pain game. Now would be a good time to go back and write out a green index card for yourself if you haven't already.

▶ **Limiting your perspective** and blaming yourself perpetuates suffering. Your nervous system plays a big role. Say out loud, "It's not me, it's my nervous system" and notice the effect that has on you.

▶ **Importance of being present.** What environments, thoughts or activities pull you out of the present moment? What can you do to take your power back?

CHAPTER SEVEN

Identity and Human Needs

*"The great solution to all human problems
is individual inner transformation."*
VERNON HOWARD

There is a complex relationship between identity, pain and unmet needs. Individuals often hold onto identities that involve pain because they serve some positive purpose, even if the pain itself is unpleasant. It explores the conflict between the need for belonging and the need for authenticity, showing how societal norms can impact one's sense of self. Our perception of pain and our identity can deeply affect our healing journey. Shifting identities and exploring new perspectives can open pathways to healing, allowing individuals to move beyond pain-centric identities toward more empowered and curious outlooks, ultimately leading to better overall well-being.

Renée is someone who often has hiccups. I (Wilene) rarely have hiccups. These different body experiences drive different identities and two different people. Identities can sometimes change with effort and interventions.

Since I didn't like having the hiccups, I found a technique that supported me in getting rid of them. As I applied visualization and breath strategy over time, my hiccups went away almost entirely. I now rarely get the hiccups.

Renée was born with the hiccups. She got them all the time as a kid. It made her family laugh a lot, and it even brought some much needed comic relief to the heavy sadness of her mother's funeral. She takes pleasure in this identity as someone who has the hiccups. One day during the writing of this book, Renée got the hiccups and I offered to teach her my strategy on how to get rid of them.

I (Renée) realized that even though my hiccups were loud, obnoxious and painful, I didn't actually want to get rid of them. I wasn't ready to release that identity and all the positive chemicals that go with it. I love the fun memories and stories that come with my hiccup identity. Even though they are quite painful, I don't want the joy that comes with them to go away.

Sometimes we, or our nervous system, will choose to keep or hold onto an identity even if that identity includes pain, because the net gain is more positive than negative. The sensation of hiccups is actually extremely painful, but the overall benefit from it is bigger than that moment of pain. So I choose to keep that pain. Now I could choose to not keep the hiccups, as Wilene offered to show me, but I'm just not ready and don't want to change. That's okay. Readiness for change takes time, compassion and it's probably best to not make your own readiness wrong (unless you want to suffer more).

Let's explore other factors that can often hide and keep us in pain. Renée is not willing to let go of her hiccup identity because it meets human needs of belonging, love and connection. I was willing to get rid of my hiccup identity because it met my need of physical comfort. Identities (conscious and subconscious) can keep us in pain or get us out of pain, depending on their underlying needs that are met by that identity.

Growing up, I (Wilene) had some dictates on who I was supposed to be, and I identified at the time as LGBTQ, which was outside of our family's belief system. Being authentic is a need, yet for me to be authentic conflicted with the need to belong and relate to my family. I feel incredibly blessed that I had therapeutic support, but ultimately, I realized that underneath my need to belong, I was looking to fulfill a need for approval from my family. But, they weren't able to give approval because they needed to stay authentic to their identified belief system.

I was demonstrating a common conflict: The need to belong and to be authentic. People often experience rejection by family and friends

if they are authentically true to who they are and what they are thinking, feeling and believing. Gabor Maté, MD, speaks in depth to this
dilemma in his work. In our experience, this internal conflict can be a
significant contributor to pain, disease and health anxieties.

Our culture has many belief systems of what is acceptable, normal
and okay. Which means, if your authentic self happens to fall outside
of society's stated norms, you will face conflict in getting your needs
met by society. This is clearly evidenced in studies that show disparities
in both healthcare and well-being for those with gender, race and so-
cioeconomic identities that fall outside of being white, wealthy, hetero-
sexual, and cisgender male. All humans have a need to be seen, heard
and celebrated. Anyone who receives societal scrutiny and disapproval
may have more indwelling barriers to thriving.

It's also more difficult to thrive for someone who confuses their
their diagnostic label with their identity. This is often seen with mental
and physical health diagnoses, where people use their diagnosis as an
identity instead of a signpost that is intended to point you in a direction of feeling better.

The pain of agreeing to any diagnosis (i.e. OCD, anxiety disorders,
ADHD, fibromyalgia, arthritis, PTSD, sleep disorders) as a permanent
identity that describes all of who you are can be life-altering, severe
and irreversible. All of these diagnoses are real, biological and chemical
altering experiences. And that is our point: They are experiences that
can end, as long as you don't hold on to them indefinitely as *who* you
are. In my (Renée) experience, escaping from a diagnosis that you have
agreed with as your identity (or others have put upon you), can even
lead to suicidal ideation. This is a tragic expression of unmet needs.
If someone is suicidal as a result of overidentification with a disorder,
that is a desperate attempt to meet their need to alleviate suffering. All
physical, emotional and social pain is real. The nervous system wants
to get its needs met at all costs.

That being said, it is possible to work through these issues and find
a sense of resolution and healing. By exploring and addressing issues
related to identity and unmet needs, you can gain a deeper understanding of yourself and your relationships and develop strategies for

managing your pain and improving your overall well-being. Healing is a natural part of being human, and you are not exempt from that. It is important to remember that it's okay to take breaks from therapy or seek additional support if needed. The most important thing is to find what works best for you and to be kind and patient with yourself as you navigate this process.

To get on the same page and agree on a clear definition, identity refers to the sense of self and how we see ourselves in relation to others. Unmet needs refer to our fundamental human needs, such as the need for love and connection, the need for autonomy and self-determination and the need for meaning and purpose. We can influence both our identity and needs once we are aware of them.

Now to meet Nora and learn from her journey in discovering part of her identity that came from a diagnosis and what she did about it.

Nora, a freelancer, had a failed knee surgery that shaped her identity into "someone with a bad knee." Despite efforts, her knee pain persisted, leading to doubt and a belief that her body couldn't be trusted. Her healthcare experiences reinforced this negative perspective, perpetuating a cycle of perceived threat in her nervous system. Her turning point came when she was reminded that healing involves more than fixing what's wrong. Shifting focus from limitations to possibilities, she asked herself, "What can I still do?" This prompted a shift in her mindset, empowering her to reclaim her life and trust in her body's healing potential. Nora's journey highlighted the importance of working on both body and mind. By questioning her beliefs and focusing on what she could do, she transformed her identity from a position of helplessness to someone with a recovering knee, opening doors to meaningful experiences. Now when she stretches and feels her knee tighten, she doesn't panic. She just puts her hands on it and works to loosen the muscles and ligaments because she is now someone who trusts her body and believes in its powerful ability to heal. Nora knows it will take some time, and there's no need to rush. She trusts the

*process that her body will heal, even if she doesn't understand it all
the time.*

What kind of identity do you have, and is it helping you heal or
holding you back? Are you someone who can heal, or are you just
someone who has pain? Are you someone who trusts your body, or
are you someone who doubts your body? Are you someone who just
has anxiety and always will, or can you shift your identity narrative to
be someone who experiences anxiety more often than you would like?
Are you someone that can learn skills to take your power back from
anxiety, or is anxiety something that will just always be there and make
you miserable?

Are you someone who has a bad knee (back, neck, whatever) or
are you someone who is, like Thomas Edison, discovering 10,000 ways
that knees (or back, neck, whatever) don't heal? You can question and
challenge old identities, you can ask yourself new questions and tell
new stories. Your brain will naturally find new solutions, perspectives
and ways out of your problems that didn't previously exist for you.

When you go the extra mile to challenge identities that are getting
in the way of your healing, it tends to have a lasting effect. Two years
after working with Nora, I checked in with her to see how things were
going. She proudly reported that she was no longer someone who suffered with knee pain and was gratefully back to her active lifestyle—
and life still happens. She said, "Weeks ago, I was running through
the snow on a nearby golf course with my husband. I fell and felt knee
pain. But the good news is that the fall did not set off the cascade of
fearful thoughts it once would have provoked. My body and I didn't
give up. Instead, I laughed!" Nora was so overjoyed with the fact that
she was out there and could run again. This enabled her to walk it off,
and then she ran some more. Nora no longer lives in that hopeless,
helpless place.

When you explore new identities, it gives you access to a new physiology within yourself. This shift in your biology creates new perspectives and possibilities that weren't previously available to you. I recently

saw proof of this in the spontaneous perspective that emerged when a patient of mine randomly said during one of our conversations, "You know, pain is a tool." I had never thought of pain like that, so I asked her to share more. She thoughtfully said, "What if it was possible that pain could be a tool that is here to help me see inside?"

Her perspective inspires us to think that, with great courage, we can all become people with a more curious outlook on pain, or any pain points in our lives. So many people suffer from 3D pain points that have become an identity that traps and blocks access to healing. Imagine if you are someone with longstanding skin issues, and you are constantly going back to the dermatologist to get something frozen off. What if you used that pain point as a tool, a floodlight pointing within yourself, to show you something useful, informative or helpful about your life? Are you creating the issue to go to the doctor for attention you may be missing in your day-to-day life? We can all be people that use pain points as a tool—your own personal frenemy that is here to help you become more aware of three dimensional unmet needs that are living in our human system. These changes in our identities are the kind of changes that last across time. Let's bring that spark of curious identity into the next chapter and explore a bit more about the unmet needs that pain is trying to help us see.

CHAPTER REFLECTIONS

▶ **Understand the role of identity in pain.** What identity do you have that is intertwined with pain? Reflect on whether certain identities contribute to your well-being or hinder your progress.

▶ **Embrace evolving identities.** Recognize that identities are not fixed. They can change over time with effort and interventions. What identity in you would support healing for you?

▶ **Consider that your body (or mind)** doesn't want to be in pain and it is doing all it can to keep you safe. What difference would that make in your body if you believed that were true? Be generous with your system, even if it's misbehaving, and assume underlying positive intent.

▶ **You can build trust within yourself.** Are you willing to consider that pain is a tool? Would you be open to the possibility that pain has an underlying positive intent to communicate a helpful message for you about your life?

▶ **Be willing to consider** that you are precious, cherished and loved exactly as you are, and this is the truest identity of who you are.

CHAPTER EIGHT

Nonviolent Communication and Unmet Needs

"Our identity is not solely defined by who we are, but also by the unmet needs that we carry within us. It is only when we acknowledge and address these needs that we can truly understand ourselves and fulfill our deepest desires."

UNKNOWN

We would like to introduce you to Marshall Rosenberg, PhD (1934-2015). He was an American psychologist, mediator, author, teacher, founder, and director of educational services for The Center for Nonviolent Communication. He grew up in Detroit surrounded by violence and had a dream to grow up and contribute to a world in a way that promoted more peace and reduced violence in the world.

When you experience prolonged negative sensations, there is commonly a natural increase in volume of the inner critic's voice in your head. If you listen to it carefully, it can be quite violent in its tone, words and attitude toward yourself. That voice is trying to solve the discomfort you are experiencing, but unbeknownst to that voice, it actually has the opposite effect on healing.

Nonviolent Communication (NVC) creates a simple breakdown of communication into two styles: The jackal and the giraffe. Similar to the binary nature of your biology, the jackal represents fear (threat), and the giraffe represents love (safety). Each has a certain way of communicating in the world. The jackal contributes to more violence, while the giraffe contributes to more peace. We have found it very helpful to apply this concept to our internal and external worlds.

Through Dr. Rosenberg's work, I (Renée) was able to understand with more clarity how the three dimensions of pain are interconnected. Physical, emotional and social pains are deeply interwoven and, in some ways, inseparable. All three types of pain are a desperate cry for attention that comes from your subconscious nervous system; pain is acting as a signal and expression of unmet needs.

According to research, it's currently believed by scientists that the vast majority of brain activity, around 95%, is unconscious. This includes a wide range of processes, such as automatic bodily functions, habits, patterns, personality traits, emotions, creativity, beliefs, values, cognitive biases, and long-term memory.

We think 95% is a lot. Your conscious mind simply cannot comprehend the magnitude of all the subconscious mind does. The unconscious mind performs 400 billion actions per second—that's too much for anyone to keep track! Let yourself off the hook and start using pain as a tool, or a flashlight, to point you toward your unmet needs instead.

Many people don't have their needs conscious on their radar of awareness. That's okay, you can become aware. The NVC model provides a helpful reference, a list of human needs. This thorough inventory is a valuable resource that you can use to empower yourself as you courageously begin using pain as a tool. Please note we aren't pretending pain is fun or pleasant, and we fully acknowledge pain is a very unpleasant tool to use, but the more you use it to your advantage, the more you take your power back from it.

Using the needs inventory (The Needs Inventory is reprinted on Page 69 with credit to Center for Nonviolent Communication © 2005. www.cnvc.org) allows you to use your pain flashlight to shine on the hidden darkness of your subconscious self. When you bring curiosity to the list of needs, it can illuminate what's hiding in your dark subconscious. It seems to spark the inner light of your innate wisdom to guide you toward what is missing in your life that the pain is trying to alert you to. Once the unmet needs are identified, you can begin the courageous process of making requests (of yourself and others) to get your needs met in a more empowering way.

Human needs are natural, normal and healthy. They are not an indicator of weakness. They are an indicator of your humanity. When you use pain as a tool, you consider pain as an alarm signal, like a dashboard indicator, letting you know what's going on under the hood of your consciousness. This list of human needs is like a manual similar to the car manual you can reference when a dashboard light comes on. There is an acronym for pain: Pay Attention Inside Now. This list of human needs shows you how to Pay Attention Inside Now acting as a headlamp to a dark space within that might be unfamiliar to you.

This needs inventory, paradoxically, is a list that helps you become more aware of your condition as an expression of unmet needs and an attempt at resolution. Your system is simply doing its best to try to get its needs met. It's willing to do whatever it takes, even if it locks you in a prison of pain, unhappiness or perpetual doctor visits.

The list of needs is neither exhaustive nor definitive. It is offered for you to use as a guide—a starting place to provoke thought and curiosity. Greater awareness is the key that unlocks the door to new choices and helps you walk out of the stuck identity cage you have been living in.

When I started working with Wilene, I was witnessing a woman in a tremendous amount of suffering and reacting to her pain from a jackal perspective. Jackal energy, as defined within NVC, is demonstrated by judgments, blame, "shoulds," perceptions, expectations, and no choices. This is natural and common—many people with an accumulation of unmet needs respond to their pain from a reactionary jackal standpoint. One of the most important parts of my job is to view someone's pain and jackal physiology from a giraffe perspective, and then guide them to learn how to do the same. When we respond to pain (in ourselves or another) from a giraffe perspective, choice, connection, intention, and freedom are available. This is brought about by engaging with more objective observations about one's experience, being curious about needs and feelings, and making requests (of ourselves or another) to get needs met.

From my giraffe perspective, most of Wilene's physical symptoms seemed to have a more emotional driver behind them and her physical pain was acting as an alarm of unmet needs. The more of her story she shared, we discovered unmet needs of support, safety, compassion, and empathy. Marshall Rosenberg uses the giraffe as an archetype for love and safety because of its tall overhead view and seven-pound heart. I felt called to show up and lead with giraffe kindness and love because Wilene was already beating herself up from new age, spiritual teachings that had trained her to believe her manifestations of her pain were all her fault. She had also been beaten up through the psychological healthcare system that had not linked the mind-body connection for her, reinforcing she was broken and couldn't be fixed. Always seeking the next guru, book or seminar, the last thing she needed from me was further critical condemnation. She needed compassion, understanding and a new perspective of what was going on.

Now is a good time for you to look at the Needs Inventory on page 69. Do you have any unmet needs? What is missing for you in your body, mind, relationships, workplace, and/or at home? To be seen and heard is a natural, normal need. It's necessary for you to feel safe, connected and like you belong. Sometimes you need to trust your instincts and speak up, even if it's uncomfortable! Ask yourself and trusted others questions to ensure that you are receiving the best care possible.

CONNECTION
acceptance
affection
appreciation
belonging
cooperation
communication
closeness
community
companionship
compassion
consideration
consistency
empathy
inclusion
intimacy
love
mutuality
nurturing
respect/
self-respect
safety
security
stability

CONNECTION *continued*
support
to know and be known
to see and be seen
to understand and be understood
trust
warmth

PHYSICAL WELL-BEING
air
food
movement/exercise
rest/sleep
sexual expression
safety
shelter
touch
water

HONESTY
authenticity
integrity
presence

PLAY
joy
humor

PEACE
beauty
communion
ease
equality
harmony
inspiration
order

AUTONOMY
choice
freedom
independence
space
spontaneity

MEANING
awareness
celebration of life
challenge
clarity
competence
consciousness
contribution
creativity
discovery
efficacy
effectiveness
growth
hope
learning
mourning
participation
purpose
self-expression
stimulation
to matter
understanding

I was fortunate to have met Renée at the beginning of my physical pain journey. Until I met her, no one had connected my decades of emotional pain and unmet needs that were now showing up physically.

I was very familiar with emotional pain, but not as much with physical pain. However, I spent a lifetime in the mental healthcare system. I had been in therapy since I was fourteen, and I was still seeking those answers, feeling helpless and powerless.

The physical healthcare system can often reinforce learned helplessness in its consumers; that was also true for me in the mental healthcare system. Neither healthcare system, whether mental or physical, had ever given me the emotional release I was looking for.

Getting those emotional core needs met went a long way in bringing a healing balm to the decades of emotional suffering that was recently identified and showing up as physical pain. Even as I sit here writing this, I am experiencing one of my most common physical pains in my left hip and lower back. My previous jackal response would have been to tighten up and hold my shoulders under my ears. I learned from Renée how to respond to my pain more like a giraffe, get curious and make observations of how my emotional pain was showing up as physical pain.

What was fascinating to me (Renée), was that when Wilene's back and hip pain showed up while writing this chapter together, there was nothing objectively or physically dangerous happening in the moment. Simply writing about old emotional pain was sufficient excitation of her nervous system and the activation of its alarm signal to create an experience of physical pain.

My (Wilene) pain was very real, and when we both brought our giraffe perspective to my pain, I was able to see the underlying connection of a painful past childhood experience that didn't receive the compassion it needed and deserved. My physical pain was here to bring my attention to a stored childhood experience that was traumatic. I realized, through a giraffe perspective, that my present physical pain was how my body was processing a past experience when I was a nine-year-old victim of violence. On some level, we all process the emotional experiences through the physical body through a mechanism called Emotional Motor Programs. As I learned from my back and hip pain, every feeling—conscious or not—has a corresponding physical expression in the body.

The pain showed up for me to learn something. Even though I was a victim at that moment as a nine-year-old, I learned there were things I could do and actions I could take today. Renée started teaching me exercises to show compassion for the pain by stretching (as opposed to stretching to "fix and get rid of"). The physical pain, even though it was driven by an emotional unmet need, still needs physical attention and care. There is a different kind of physical effect that occurs when we do the physical intervention with an underlying awareness of the emotional needs. You still need to address the physical, but your outcome will be more effective when you do so with an underlying awareness of the psychological drivers underneath. It becomes your job to pamper the pain after finding the mental causes and then doing what you need physically to show compassion to your nervous system and its needs. Knowing there is something you can do brings hope to an overwhelming situation.

Learning how to respond to your pain like a giraffe instead of a jackal is likely not something that comes naturally. You weren't meant to learn how to be with pain and suffering alone. If your life circumstances dictated that you had to be alone with pain, it's natural that your system has a jackal reaction to pain. That's biologically appropriate because needing support in a state of pain is normal. Yet sadly, many of us had to learn to be with pain alone, which is why many have such strong fear (jackal) responses to pain. The jackal in your system will tense up around the pain and keep you stuck in the pain. Humans are meant to heal in relationship and community. The jackal response of tension can learn from others how to be like the giraffe instead. This allows the nervous system to relax and get its needs met so the pain alarm signals can stop ringing.

Responding to pain from a giraffe perspective instead of jackal is a skill that requires courage, practice, guidance, and support. Initially, many people need a lot of support, but with time, they can learn to do it alone. This was beautifully demonstrated in Bertie, a 72-year-old retired educator with "arthritic" knee pain.

Bertie's x-rays showed she needed a knee replacement. After eight weeks of working with me through a very holistic body-mind approach, her knee pain was 90% resolved. One night she woke with throbbing knee pain at 3am, panicked and did all of her physical exercises to no avail. Her immediate jackal reaction (fear) was to panic and think she was going to need a knee replacement after all. Luckily, she was able to take a breath and find her calm, curious giraffe perspective within. This enabled her to scour her thoughts through a scientific, 3D tracking approach. She realized that contrary to her catastrophic fear-based jackal feelings, maybe she didn't need a knee replacement at all. Perhaps she was simply dehydrated from seven hours of walking around a lot earlier that day in the heat. She decided to run an experiment, stayed curious and chugged eight ounces of water. The knee pain she was told would only resolve through a knee replacement surgery went away.

Wilene and Bertie learned to listen to their pain (Pay Attention Inside Now) with a more curious, observing giraffe perspective. Now they respond to old pains in a new way. This enabled them to become their own advocate and their confidence grew as they were more effective. This empowered them in the face of pain, rather than reinforced the learned helplessness that can so often show up in the presence of overwhelming pain or whatever the unpleasant condition is. Your newfound giraffe awareness and knowledge, guided by your instinct, will bolster your confidence to journey more boldly to the unknown landscape within you.

We all have jackal doubts, insecurities and fears, which is normal, healthy and makes you human. It's important to remember that it's not all that you are. There is a giraffe perspective in you, even if you feel disconnected from it. Just because you cannot see it right now doesn't mean it doesn't exist.

It's easy to become so identified with unhelpful, fear-based collective belief systems that we can't see we are in them, just like a fish doesn't know it's in water. Some common beliefs are: It sucks to get old, this pain in life is just the way it is, I am sick, I have a bad back, and life sucks. All of those things can be true for all of us at some points in time, but that doesn't mean that is all there is. Just like there are fears, doubts and insecurities, there is wisdom, knowing, instinct, and our intuition. We lose sight of those resources within us when we are caught up in fears, insecurities and doubts. This is not unlike a cat in a carrier with the rooftop window open. They can only see the closed door in front of them and think they are locked in, totally oblivious to the way out just above them. When we are only focused and fixated on the problem, solutions evade us. We all can get caught up in unhelpful jackal collective belief systems. And we can all remember the giraffe possibilities that can still exist—that aging is a privilege, my body is healing and life doesn't have to suck all the time.

**When we are only focused and fixated
on the problem, solutions evade us.**

CHAPTER REFLECTIONS

▶ **Pain is a tool.** Would you be willing to consider pain as your own personal frenemy? It's here to act as an alert system for unmet needs, signaling your attention to aspects of consciousness that need attention.

▶ **Nonviolent Communication (NVC).** Where do you communicate like a jackal (fear-based)? With whom do you relate like a giraffe (love-based)? How would you apply this concept to your communication to foster more peaceful outcomes?

▶ **Needs Inventory.** Use the Inventory of Human Needs to empower yourself. What are your unmet needs in various aspects of your life, such as body, mind, relationships, and work? What needs are you already meeting? Celebrate what you already are doing well.

▶ **Let go.** Remember that around 95% of brain activity is unconscious. Give yourself permission to not have to control and/or understand all of the neurons in your system.

CHAPTER NINE

DIMs, SIMs and Pulse Checks

*"Safety is not the absence of threat, it
is the presence of connection."*
GABOR MATÉ, M.D.

Up until now, we have explored various scientific research and stories that challenge, inform and reframe our thinking about unpleasant circumstances and conditions. Changing your thinking is good, but it's not all there is. You need a balance of change in your thinking, feeling and behaving to generate lasting change. We will explore some tangible, actionable strategies you can start putting into practice.

As you learn, practice and incorporate new habits and behaviors, you can celebrate because the changes you're making will be resting on a new, sustainable foundation of thought. It's good news! You are behaving in a way that will lead to lasting and positive change in your life.

If you have a bank account where you keep money, you know that if you make more withdrawals than deposits, you'll go broke. It's the same with the nervous system in our bodies. If it has more stress responses than relaxation responses, you go broke. In other words, if you have more circuits of threat than safety, you "go broke" somewhere in the form of a breakdown in your health and/or well-being.

Did you know that if you laid out your nervous system in a straight line, it would extend the distance of 44 miles? Were you aware of the fact that your nervous system is composed of 100 billion neurons and can create 100 trillion possibilities of connection? That's incredible! Stop and think about that for a moment.

The good news of that is that virtually anything is possible within you. The tricky news is that it depends on how your brain's threat detection system is wired. This involves many regions of your nervous system and their subconscious wiring patterns. One of these regions includes the fairly well known amygdala in your limbic system, or emotional brain. The amygdala is a paired structure, meaning there are two of them—one on each side of your brain. It plays a big role in your threat detection system and contributes to the subconscious decisions that are made on a moment to moment, context-specific basis, as to whether or not your physical person is in any potential danger. If this threat detection system decides (without your conscious control or awareness) that there is some sort of physical, emotional and/or social threat related to your survival, your circuits of threat and defense will become activated. Again, this is not something you decide; threat circuits get activated often and this happens below the screen of your radar and conscious awareness.

By often, we mean 50-100 times per day, at a minimum. That likely means your nervous system is running more circuits of threat than you realize, activating programs within you that are running from a perceived place of fear, making you defend and protect yourself in ways you don't even realize. This secretly builds up a physiological bank account within your biological human system that is biased towards circuits of threat or danger. This is the underground biological driver of all dis-ease in mind and body.

To be better able to track your physiological bank account balance, we find it helpful to think about a little play on words that was created by the Neuro-Orthopedic Institute (NOI). The clever folks over at NOI, created a word play on Dim Sum, a traditional Chinese meal.

DIMs and SIMs

Instead of puffy little dough balls, they created the words DIM SIM, and no, that's not a typo. DIM and SIM are clever acronyms that stand for Danger In Me and Safety In Me. There are seven categories of DIMs and SIMs. See the chart for some examples. This is the bank account balance you are trying to shift. When you have more SIMs than DIMs, according to logic, math and science, your pain will be eliminated. Somewhere in your system, conscious or not, if you have more DIMs than SIMs, you will continue to experience pain. It really is that simple. And please hear us correctly: We are not suggesting this is easy. The intention is to give you some concrete, actionable things you can do. Most people notice a subtle, yet powerful shift after a few weeks. This is because they are behaving in a way that is adjusting the ratio of their SIMs to DIMs, toward an ever-increasing balance of more SIMs than DIMs.

Categories	DIM examples	SIM examples
Things you hear, see, smell, touch, taste	Looking at MRI findings, sounds at the dentist	Hearing your test results are clear, loving cuddles with fur pals
Things you do	Wait and hope for someone to "fix" you, stay at home all the time	Move your body, get outside, learn skills to care for your body
Things you say	"It sucks to get old," "I've got fibromyalgia"	"This sucks, but it's going to be okay," "This is figure-outtable, let me see what I can do"
Things you think and believe	"I can't," "I'm afraid this won't change," "This is just the way it is, there's nothing I can do"	"I'm willing to be open," "Tissues can heal, trauma can end," "I can feel happier," "It's going to be okay"
Places you go	Hospital, surgeon's office	Nature walk with my bestie
People in your life	Messy housemate, a dismissive health care provider, critical parent, depressed spouse	Friends who understand and don't judge me, health care provider I trust and like
Things happening in your body	Unpleasant and/or painful sensations, acute inflammation	Pleasant and/or safe sensations, acute inflammation

These examples, as every example, can be a DIM, SIM or both. All examples are completely dependent on context (external circumstances and the meaning you make of them)

In my exploration of creating more SIMs, I (Wilene) started practicing some simple exercises and techniques to begin healing. When I developed more SIMs in my bank account, more synchronicities began to appear. Living with more safety in me increased my ability to allow new ideas, inspiration and follow my intuition with more clarity and confidence. Do not underestimate the power of consistent, repetitive, seemingly small actions built upon a foundation of safety. Long-term change doesn't happen from one giant leap to fixing everything. It happens through tiny shifts in your thinking, feeling and behavior that accumulate over time.

It's true that small steps can often be more important than big ones in the process of healing and personal growth. By focusing on small, manageable actions, it can be easier to make and see progress, which can be motivating and help build momentum. Remind yourself frequently that long-term change doesn't happen overnight. For some, long-term change can take longer than you want. You may get frustrated, think it's not working and want to give up. Many people are so sick and tired of their present circumstances that they try to make sweeping changes all at once. This is an effective way to sabotage yourself and stay miserable. But, you can make progress and create lasting change in your life.

Dan, a 34-year-old tech entrepreneur, struggled with neck pain and dizziness from vestibular neuritis for a decade despite various treatments. With an imminent trip to Tibet, he feared his symptoms would flare up and ruin the experience. Recognizing his response pattern to dizziness as a fear-based neurological reaction, he decided it was time for a change. In just two sessions, Dan learned new strategies. By focusing on awareness and practicing a simple exercise called Slow Blinking, he experienced noticeable relief. He realized the tension he held in his face and hands exacerbated his symptoms. Slow Blinking, an easy tool that countered panic responses, helped him feel more in control. Dan's breakthrough came during his trip when he faced dizziness on the plane. Instead of panic, he used the techniques he learned, and the dizziness resolved within minutes. For the first time in a decade, he felt empowered and in control of his symptoms. It was a significant turning point, showing him the power of responding to a distressing sensation (DIM) with a calming action (SIM). This process, although quick for Dan, might take longer for others. However, the hope lies in the simplicity of recognizing distressing sensations and responding differently. Dan's experience taught him that change doesn't always require a superhero; it's about incremental steps toward empowerment and shifting from distress to a calmer response.

One of the most important ways you can increase SIMs is to practice greater awareness of what is happening in and around your human system. Like Dr. Phil says, "You can't change it if you aren't aware of it." Awareness was the first and most important step for Dan, and many others, and will be for you, too.

China has one of the world's oldest medical systems. Acupuncture and Chinese herbal remedies have been around for at least 2,200 years. That's a lot of time devoted to discovering what works and what doesn't. That's a lot of time to develop awareness of the human system and what it needs to be well. While we are not trained in Chinese medicine, we respect it and all that it can do to promote health and optimize well-being.

When a traditionally western trained healthcare provider checks your pulse, they generally will collect one piece of information about your body—your heart rate. On the other hand, when a Chinese medicine Master Acupuncturist checks your pulse, they can collect data on up to 28 different body systems through what is called a Pulse Diagnosis. That's 28 times more data than what a western trained provider will collect about your system. In other words, the Master Acupuncturist is highly trained in knowing and understanding what is happening inside your body.

Pulse Checks

We want to help you in developing your skills to become more versed at knowing and understanding what is happening in your body through what we like to call a Pulse Check. A pulse check, like the Pulse Diagnosis, trains you to get into the habit of paying attention to your own human system. When the Master Acupuncturist is paying attention to one thing (your pulse), they are gathering data on different body systems. You, like the Master Acupuncturist, can attend to one thing (your own human system) and gather different pieces of information. You are learning how to pay deeper attention to your own body, breath and emotional motor programs. The more data you have, the more experiments you can run and the more you can discover about what works uniquely for you and your own blueprint for greater fulfillment, joy, health, and peace.

When you pay more curious attention to yourself, you are generating more SIMs within you. Doing frequent pulse checks throughout the day—every 20 to 60 minutes—builds the habit of you becoming a Master in the Awareness of your own human system, which affects your health, mind and overall life.

What does a pulse check look like exactly? Simply stated, a pulse check is bringing your attention and awareness to yourself for a moment in time. It's an exercise that creates a new foundation within yourself to stand solidly upon. Pulse checks invite you into a level of self-awareness that may not be familiar to you. With continued practice, they can become second nature.

B&B Pulse Check

As we mentioned earlier, there are different kinds of pulse checks. You'll start here with a B&B (Breath & Body) Pulse Check. It's taking 10-12 seconds of your awareness and with exquisitely focused attention to the fact that you actually have a body. Most of us don't pay attention to our body unless there is something wrong. With a B&B Pulse Check, we are asking you to bring attentional focus to your body and breath, not because there is something wrong but because you want to start building a relationship with your breath and body *as it is,* at any given moment. This builds trust and safety between you and your body. This promotes SIMs in you.

Taking 10-12 seconds of your attention may feel like a really long time at first. It may also feel initially weird or unfamiliar to notice the felt sense of your body with its container of skin and all the things happening inside of it. Pay attention to pleasant, neutral and unpleasant sensations. Notice what feels both good and bad. Get curious about the level of energy that exists in your system—does it feel low, medium or high? As you build the habit of checking in with your body, your body can start behaving like a happy little kid that is finally getting the lollipop it's been wanting. Checking in is a way of soothing the temper tantrum that your body is throwing because it hasn't been getting enough attention.

So, take a moment now and recognize what's going on with your body. Are your shoulders under your ears? Are your muscles tense or relaxed? What is happening in and around your stomach, hands, neck, shoulders, jaw, feet, shins, and thighs. Is your breath deep or shallow? How deep does your breath go? Does it go down to your chest, stomach or pelvis? Can you notice if the back or sides of your ribs have movement? Check in and see what's going on right now. Is your weight on one leg more than another? Are you on your toes or are your heels touching? What position is your spine and where is your head relative to the rest of your body? Are your hands clenched, tense or relaxed? You'll often notice that just paying attention can have a relaxing effect without trying, forcing or pushing to relax yourself.

When you practice awareness of your body, it begins to support you with new neural pathways of more ease and comfort. This happens because it's feeling safe knowing you are paying attention to it. Your body devlops those habits of relaxtion not through force and effort but through natural consequences of getting its needs of attention met. We all need to be seen, heard and celebrated, and that includes your body.

CHAPTER REFLECTIONS

- **DIMs and SIMs can all change with awareness.** Pay attention to the seven categories of DIMs and SIMs in your life. Simply becoming aware can act as a powerful catalyst to change danger (fear) to safety (love/connection).

- **Don't mistake simple tools for ineffective or unimpressive.** Notice tension patterns in your body (hands, eyes, mouth, tongue, neck, shoulders, and legs) throughout the day. Choose to intentionally relax them. No one is making them tense but you.

- **Perform regular pulse checks** every 20-60 minutes. Spend 10-12 seconds bringing your attention to your breath and body. Notice sensations, tension, relaxation, and the level of energy in your body.

CHAPTER TEN

Stress Responses

*"Although the world is full of suffering, it is full
also of the overcoming of it. My optimism,
then, does not rest on the absence of evil,
but on a glad belief in the preponderance of
good and a willing effort always to cooperate
with the good, that it may prevail."*

HELEN KELLER

For you to have a more complete understanding of your present-day sensations, you need to take a look not just at your tissues and diagnoses, but also evaluate potential toxic and/or incomplete stress responses in your life (both past and present) and how they impact the way you perceive the world.

As you do pulse checks, you're paying attention to your body. Technically, the body is the only thing that is present to the here and now. That being said, your body can also be an expression of past experiences—both good and bad. It's ironic how the present moment of your body can serve as a window to the past.

When I (Wilene) was in elementary school, my sister and I were fishing with our grandfather. The peaceful outing turned chaotic when my sister stepped on an underground bumblebee hive. Thousands of bees (not kidding—we're lucky we're not allergic) began stinging us. As we ran, people were screaming, "Jump in the water!" Everything ended up okay after our mom put bacon fat all over us. But the experience registered as fear and stayed in my nervous system. For many years, I had body tension and a flight response when I saw bees, wasps or literally any flying insects. Nearly 10 years later, I was mowing the lawn and saw a bumblebee. I let go of the lawn mower, which continued to the neighbor's yard, and ran to my mother crying. Mom asked, "Did it sting you? I said, "No, it just scared me." That was the day I decided I would not live with that fear anymore. I began consciously staying still and noticing my breath when a bee was around and would repeat, "It won't hurt me if I don't hurt it." I was able to release the intensity of the fear. I still have to be conscious not to run, but my awareness of the fear allows me to make conscious decisions around my response.

My sister has a bigger fear sense, which was passed on to her children. Even though they've never experienced being stung, they are terrified of bees, wasps and other flying insects. My sister and I both experienced the same event. As a result of different fear responses around that event, we generated different outcomes in our lives. My present-day body can be relaxed around flying insects while my sister has a body that tenses. Fear is contagious, and we can all make choices about how we want to show up in the face of it, once we are aware of it. The body is an excellent indicator of where fear lives in the circuits of our nervous system.

Wilene and her sister demonstrate a wonderful example here of recognizing an incomplete stress response. As an adult, Wilene recognizes she was having an exaggerated response to the stimulus of a bee. She was able to complete her stress response by breathing and telling herself, "It won't hurt me, if I don't hurt it." No one taught her how to do that—she figured it out on her own. That is wonderful, credible evidence that the ability to heal lies naturally within us.

You can learn to discover and close the loop on any physiological incomplete stress responses that lie hidden underground in the subconscious of your own nervous system. It's simple, but not necessarily always easy. Just notice and curiously observe your own behaviors. Any time you watch yourself having an exaggerated response to a life stimulus, that is an objective indicator of a hidden and incomplete physiological stress response. An exaggerated startle response, like flying off the handle at a barking dog or a huge pile of laundry, may be telling you something about what's below the surface of your conscious self. If you find yourself completely losing your cool over the toilet seat being left up or crumbs on the countertop, that is a good sign that there is at least one circuit of unresolved stress in your nervous system.

Sensations we experience in the body now, including pain, can sometimes be an expression of an incomplete stress response from the past. We have discovered together how pain isn't always just coming from physical and tissue damage. It can be a more complex syndrome that is related to threats you perceive in your life, both past and present.

For some of you, this can mean taking a look at your past, because what happened to your nervous system as a child can interrupt, dysregulate and throw your normal healing systems offline. It's still remarkable to me (Renée) how the loss of my mom as a child over 30 years ago, can grip and take over my present-day breathing patterns when I feel sad, elicit a freeze response in the face of present day overwhelm and wreak havoc on my gut when I am feeling stressed, afraid or worried.

Childhood plays a biological and physical role in how our brains and bodies develop. Our inner voice can continue that same dynamic without us realizing it. That means that even if our present-day environments aren't necessarily toxic, we can perceive them as such because of the way our brain is wired. As a result, we can misperceive our surroundings and our inputs. Benign strangers can become threats. Friendly gestures can be misinterpreted. Malcolm Gladwell's book, *Talking to Strangers*, is a fascinating read about this concept. Studies show that children who have been abused often have trouble actually reading a friendly face from an abusive one. This tells us that it's not just the present-day environment we surround ourselves with that has an effect. It's also the very way we perceive the world in our mind's eye that also plays a role.

The learned behaviors from your past will dictate how your operating system drives you to experience your present-day life. My learned behavior of feeling hopeless from losing my mom at age 11, affects my confidence and optimism as a business owner today at age 45. You may or may not believe that past childhood experiences can have powerful impacts on present day body and health. And luckily, you don't need to believe us. We can lean into some scientific research here.

The ACE Study conducted by Kaiser Permanente and the CDC uncovered a strong connection between childhood trauma and later health problems. It analyzed 10 types of trauma, categorized as personal and family-related, among over 17,000 participants. These adverse childhood experiences often occurred together, increasing the risk for chronic diseases, mental illness and violence. ACEs were found to heighten the likelihood of smoking and alcoholism and significantly impacted lifespan.

Contrary to assumptions about poverty, the study primarily involved white, educated, middle-class individuals. Childhood adversity contributes to toxic stress, impacting a child's development and long-term well-being. However, one isn't trapped in a victim role; altering the story we tell ourselves about our past can shape its influence on our present.

For example, a person shares how different aspects of their childhood story shift their perspective from feeling burdened to hopeful. The ACEs quiz outcomes vary based on our subjective assessment of our past. Someone from a middle-class background realized their perceived childhood shifted from good to feeling like a war zone refugee based on how they answered.

This experience illustrates the power of choice in shaping one's life perception. Embracing a higher ACEs score led to more negative emotions, while a slightly lower score opened up possibilities for well-being. This shift enabled alignment with the desired identity in various roles.

The study's findings emphasize how altering our view of the past significantly impacts present and future well-being. Our interpretation of the past and the details we focus on influence our responses to the ACEs questions. Life's nuances and subjectivity are evident in cases like Wilene's, where feeling unprotected, despite having basic needs met, affected her ACEs score.

Additionally, observations about individuals on death row revealed a common history of childhood abuse and high ACE scores above four. Inspiring figures with challenging childhoods demonstrate that a positive life and impact on others are achievable, irrespective of past adversity.

One way you can affect your past is to become aware of what memories and what part of each memory you focus on. I (Renée) see many people focus on the part of the story that is problematic, rather than on the resolution of the story. This is not a character flaw but rather a product of our biology and millions of years of evolution. For example, I unknowingly perpetuated my own victim mentality from the time I was 13 when I perceived my dad humiliating me in public. For years, that bad part of the memory is what stood out to me.

When I started to challenge my own neural circuits and memory, I realized that I was consumed by the part of the story that sucked, not the good part of the story. I had inadvertently wired in the bad stuff. When I recognized that and paid more attention to the good part of the story, I found resolution, love and peace with how my sister recognized my sadness after the public humiliation and came to comfort me by giving me a giggle cookie. When I shifted the attention from the bad part of the memory to the good part of the memory, I was able to wire in the good and lessen the effects of the bad.

What I mean by "wiring in" a memory refers to the process of establishing a strong neural connection in the brain to a specific memory so that it becomes firmly embedded and easily retrievable. This can happen through repetition and reinforcement of the memory, or by connecting it to strong emotional or sensory experiences. The result is a wired-in memory that can be easily recalled and influences future behavior and thought patterns.

I wired in the more unpleasant part of the story by paying more attention to it. I received the negative expressions in my nervous system, and neck pain when I was around another male that came across to me as intimidating or humiliating. As I paid more attention and felt in my body the good part of the story, I felt so much better. I wasn't invalidating the hard stuff I went through. Rather I shifted my focus and took my power back by noticing, remembering, feeling, and celebrating that someone was there to notice me, care for me and provide love. That yielded a much happier chemical state of my nervous system, relationships, perspectives, and life because I no longer needed to be a victim of my past. Changing the part of the story I focused on allowed me to shift my nervous system from a powerless, helpless victim into an empowered creator that can rewrite my present through changing how I look at my past.

What are some key memories in your past that occupy your mind circuits frequently? Are your circuits fixating on what's bad, wrong and unsafe about it? Are you stuck in the unsafe problem part of the story? If so, that's okay. It's good to be aware of and then challenge yourself to get curious. What's good, safe and correct about that narrative? When did the problem end or get better? What made it better? Can you find a felt sense of that peaceful goodness within you?

This can be challenging, and thankfully humans are resilient. The more you work this muscle, the more capable you become in the face of challenges and the sometimes inevitable suck in life that comes along with being human. This exercise is a wonderful opportunity for that, and you'll reap the added benefit of feeling more confident in the face of things that you're afraid of.

CHAPTER REFLECTIONS

▸ **Shift your focus** when revisiting past memories or experiences. Challenge yourself to shift your focus from the negative or problematic aspects to the positive or empowering ones. Identify moments of resolution, growth or support within those memories.

▸ **Work on reframing** the stories you tell about your past. Instead of dwelling on the negative aspects, emphasize the moments of strength, resilience and growth. This can reshape how you perceive your past and influence your present mindset.

▶ **The past is a place to learn from**, not live in. What good things about your upbringing do you want to cherish, celebrate and perpetuate? Take a stand and make an active choice to rebel against that which no longer serves you, while keeping that which does.

CHAPTER ELEVEN

Drama and Empowered Triangle Roles

*"I'm still learning to love the parts
of me that no one claps for."*
RUDY FRANCISCO

As you begin to reclaim yourself from your painful past and stop allowing those circuits to create a painful future, it's helpful to look at some common personal and interpersonal dynamics that can play a role in keeping you in a cycle of pain. It's a good time to look at how you're interacting with others, to begin to pull yourself into a powerful, peaceful and present state of now.

Many people become chemically, neurologically and/or socially stuck in a drama triangle. If this happens to you, you'll get caught up in conflict which locks you into self-satisfying and self-punishing roles that limit your ability to reconnect your mind to your body and your body to your mind.

The Drama Triangle

Dr. Stephen Karpman, as a young psychiatrist in the late 1960s and early 1970s, formulated the theory of this pathological drama triangle in relationships and how they embroil us in constant conflict with our psyche and the psyches of others. He defined three roles in how we often orient ourselves to others. There is the Persecutor. There is the Rescuer. And there is the Victim.

The Persecutor is the one that is controlling, dogmatic and rigid. They'll say, "I'm right, and you're wrong," "You need to get straight and right now" and "It's all your fault." These people feel inadequate underneath and feel the need to control with threats, order and rigidity. Take a moment to notice or imagine how that energy, from another or within yourself, might affect your body.

The Rescuer is an enabler. This person needs to help, often losing a sense of self in continually bailing out others. They'll say, "I can do it for you," "I can take care of that" and "I can figure it out for you." They say "yes" when they should say "no." This person keeps others in a dependent role and focuses outward on others. In focusing on others, this person rarely looks inward. Can you recall a time you showed up as a Rescuer? Can you remember a time where someone tried to rescue you, even when you didn't need it? Notice what sensations show up in your body.

The Victim says to the world, "Poor me." This person feels powerless and struggles to find pleasure in life. They'll say, "I can't," "Can't you just fix me," "Why do things never go my way," or "You always make this so difficult for me." It's always about the blame game. Others are at fault and this person takes no ownership of what is happening in their own lives. They feel helpless, hopeless and unable to act or empower themselves. As you imagine this expression in yourself or another, how are you holding your body? What is your posture and how are you breathing?

As we negotiate our relationships with others, we often fluctuate among these roles, shifting into a different stance depending on where our emotions are pulling us and how the other person is interacting with us. We can get pulled from one type of personality into another just by getting overloaded with all the stimulus one personality can provoke. For instance, a person acting as a Persecutor can eventually collapse and become a Victim crying out that nobody ever heeds their advice or listens to them. Or a Rescuer can get worn out from all the energy spent on others and suddenly feel like a Victim whose needs get ignored. A Victim can get mad at the perpetual negative messages and lack of power they hear from a Persecutor. Suddenly, that Victim can rise up and switch to the Persecutor role. Even with these fluctuations, we tend to gravitate toward one role or another. Usually, these roles come from the way we oriented ourselves in our childhood. For us, we both became the Rescuers of a Victim parent. We tend to revert to the roles we learned as children, the roles our family dynamics taught us. What's your most familiar role when life stress is coming on strong?

Here's a sample dialogue:

Husband comes home after a long day of work to find the dinner burning.

"Honey, you never get anything right. Do we need to send you back to your mother to learn how to serve a proper meal?" He's acting as the typical Persecutor here.

Wife replies: "I do everything around here. Little Wendy wanted me to stop on the way home from work and pick up makeup and had a list a mile long for snacks. So I was rushing." The wife is acting the Rescuer here.

"Nobody ever takes care of me." Wife is acting as the Victim.

Husband: "Our daughter needs to learn to take care of herself. This is a joke. She's 14. She's not going to have anyone running errands when she's a grownup." Husband still is acting as Persecutor.

Wife: "You stop picking on her. She needs her childhood. She needs to know someone loves her in this world." Wife is acting as a Rescuer.

Husband: "You need to learn to take care of yourself more and stop worrying about her. You need to focus on yourself. It's too much for you." He's playing both the Rescuer and the Persecutor here.

Husband: "Damn, I'm always working to provide a living for this family and nobody cares. What do I even have a job for? It's just living the rat race." Suddenly, he's become the Victim.

Wife: "Funny, I thought my paycheck was what allowed us to pay the utilities. You never really understand all the stuff that

I do for everyone." Suddenly, she slipped into the Victim. All her rescuing has left her defeated.

"I can cook something else. It won't take too long." She's back to being a full-blown Rescuer.

Husband: "Waste of some good hamburger meat." Persecutor.

Wife: "Well, if you would have just gotten your lazy ass into gear and picked up her makeup on the way home, we wouldn't have been so frenzied." Persecutor.

Husband: "You never told me anything about any damn makeup. It's your fault." Persecutor.

Wife: "You never even bother to call to ever ask what I need." Persecutor.

Wife: "Nobody ever cares about me." Victim.

You see how this dialogue has locked everyone into destructive roles where no one's needs are getting met? Imagine the toll that these roles take on their bodies. In fact, go ahead and do a B&B Pulse Check right now. Notice your breath and body.

As I'm writing these words, I literally notice an old, familiar pain on the left side of my neck. When I'm in a good place, I can think of pain acting on my behalf and alerting me to become aware of something I'd been unaware of.

Pain is similar to the dashboard lights on a car, as we mentioned in Chapter Eight. Without dashboard lights to indicate problems to us that we would otherwise be unaware of, small problems under the hood go unnoticed and lead to much more expensive problems. At the moment of this writing about the drama triangles, my neck pain is acting like a dashboard light in a car. My neck pain is letting me know my muscles have tightened up, my breathing became more shallow. That movement pattern doesn't provide adequate blood flow to my left arm. Like a dashboard light left ignored, bigger problems can ensue if little indicators are not paid attention to. If my muscle tension and constricted breathing continue without me noticing them as a dashboard light, I could have longer term pain problems. That tension, over time, could pinch a nerve or blood vessel, create tingling in my arm, or I may lose sensation or even strength in my arm. This neck tension while writing about drama triangle roles is acting as a wonderful cue, an alert like a dashboard light to remind me to find my breath, find my seat, find my feet, and notice the objective physical safety around and within me now. My nervous system was acting out the past drama roles, even though I'm not living in them presently. As I redirect my attention, update and train my nervous system that I'm safe now, I notice the tension in my neck settle subtly and gently down. What do you notice in you? And where do you need to orient your attention to at this moment to optimize your own safety and well-being?

You can learn to get out of these disempowered roles by developing knowledge, awareness and skills. We are grateful for David Emerald and Donna Zajonc; they have illuminated for you an easier path to learn how to shift out of the roles that keep you stuck. The TED Triangle (TED = The Empowerment Dynamic) comprises three roles that serve as an "antidote" to the Victim, Rescuer and Persecutor roles. A Victim can shift into the role of Creator, a Rescuer can shift into the role of Coach, and a Persecutor can shift into the role of Challenger. The roles of Creator, Coach and Challenger act as opposing forces to the disempowered roles, giving you more choice, new options and fresh perspectives to interact in novel ways with yourself and others.

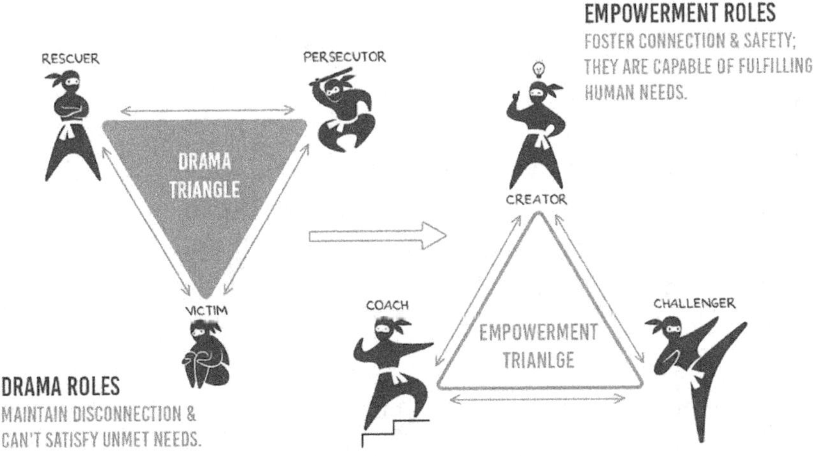

Adapted by Green Tree Mind from David Emerald, Donna Zajonc, and The Power of TED

Viktor Frankl guides us wisely, "Between stimulus and response, there is a space. In that space is our power to choose our response. In our response lies our growth and our freedom."

We can learn to inhabit the center of ourselves and our empowered triangle, as opposed to getting sucked into the drama triangle. I know I'm back in the drama triangle when I am short-tempered, impatient and frustrated. My body is tense, my breath is shallow and my face gets hijacked into a nasty grimace. Sometimes it requires every ounce of self-control I have to not pop back at the person with whom I am interacting. But I can pause, take a breath and widen the space between my response and the stimulus. Every time I do that, I increase the neurological access to my own power and shift my neuromuscular memory more into one of the Empowered Roles.

- If you're acting as the Persecutor, learn to turn it into assertive expression.
- If you are the Rescuer, learn to show real compassion.
- If you are the Victim, learn to show real vulnerability instead of just playing games.

Here's a sample dialogue of the wife and husband learning to monitor themselves and discover new ways of relating.

Wife: "You never bother to call me ever." Persecutor.
Husband: "Yes, it's true. I could get better at that."

Here the husband has flipped the switch. He's not batting down a complaint or attacking back. He's not playing one of the roles. He shifted into Creator, taking responsibility for his actions and creating the opportunity for more effective communication to take place.

It works just as well when the Victim card is being played.

Husband: "Why am I in this rat race? Nobody cares about all
    I do for this family. I'm worn out. I need some time to relax
    before I get jumped first thing after I come home." Victim.

Wife: "I'm sorry you're feeling so harried."

Which empowered role is the wife playing here? We don't actually know. An argument could be made for all three. She's Challenger because she's internally challenged her old familiar impulse to persecute him as a Victim. She could be Creator, because she's creating a new dynamic by choosing not to rescue the Victim. Or she could become Coach, if she were to start asking some questions to guide her husband toward more clarity around why he's feeling harried and what he could do about it, thus facilitating him into the role of Creator.

When you, as this couple demonstrate, are stuck in the reactive roles of the drama triangle, you are most likely asking yourself subconscious questions that inherently perpetuate the drama cycle. For example, if you are entrenched in the role of Victim during a challenging situation, you may notice internal dialogue along the lines of:

- Why did this happen to me?
- Why do I have all the bad luck?
- Why don't I get what other people get?

The Creator asks themselves different questions when faced with adversity. Specifically, the Creator's questions explore new opportunities and ways of seeing, such as:

- Given the situation, how might I make the most of it?
- Is there an unmet need here? What can I do to get it met?
- What is mine to do here?
- What is the most loving and compassionate thing I could say to myself right now?

The Persecutor also has entrenched thought patterns with a strong need to control and be right. Their thinking and dialogue might look more like asking the following:

- Who is to blame for this?

- I know I am right about this. Why don't they listen to me?
- How can I manipulate and get ahead in this situation?

The Challenger, in contrast to the Persecutor, lets go of the need to be right. Instead, the Challenger focuses on growth and learning, even in the face of tough or uncomfortable circumstances. A Challenger might offer:

- What is the surprise learning in this set-back?
- What is objectively true, given the situation?
- Where can I stay consistent with my values and still move forward?

Rescuers love jumping in and saving the day, even when not asked. A Rescuer will often inquire:

- How can I take your pain away?
- If I could do more, what else could I do?
- How can I fix this for you?

Instead of reinforcing dynamics with a helpless and powerless undertone, the Coach collaborates with another person by asking better questions. Empowering questions can create clarity and elicit opportunity for the power and responsibility to emerge within the other person. Rather than doing for the other person what they can do for themselves, the Coach may ask:

- What might be the gift or opportunity in the challenge you are facing?
- How could you make the most of the situation?
- What is it that you are really committed to?
- How would your wise, future self that is happy with the outcome advise you right now?

Asking different questions that are built upon curiosity and possibility will generate different answers and contribute to shifting into the empowered roles more frequently. This requires novel brain effort, since it is different than how your brain is used to firing. Any new skill often feels unfamiliar at first, maybe even unpleasant, yet we believe it's totally worth doing if you're committed to breaking out of the cycles, ruts and grooves in your nervous system that are keeping you stuck. The results you get are only as good as the questions you ask—of yourself and others. When you step more into the roles of Creator, Coach and Challenger, you can access more powerful questions in any moment.

This chapter's focus has been on the roles and how they play out in inter and intrapersonal dynamics. It's also interesting to think about how these roles play out in a bigger social sphere and impact our collective consciousness. For example, I'm (Renée) pretty darn tired from the years I have spent as a Rescuer, giving away my primal life force energy to patients who were forced into the position of Victim. As patients are cast into the Victim role, the healthcare system acts as the Persecutor and Big Pharma is the Rescuer ("Here, let's fix it. Just take this pill"). I see my own interpersonal dynamics within me reflected in a bigger world around me.

The disempowered dynamics, both within and around me, are a reflection of an energetic and ubiquitous sense of powerlessness that yields violent energy. This violent energy generates acts of violence within our nervous systems toward ourselves and others.

Some examples of violent energy can show up in overt ways, such as picking fights with loved ones, road rage or abusive relationships. There are more examples listed in the chart below. Violent energy can also show up in covert hidden ways such as self-loathing, a loud inner critic that beats you up, never feeling good enough, lack of boundaries, and people pleasing. In short, violent energy can live in all humans as a result of anything that occurs in your thinking, feeling and behavior that promotes the opposite experience of peace within you.

We don't believe that violent energy is a naturally occurring phenomenon. Humans aren't born with the capacity or desire to be violent. This energy is something that we learn from others, can be held subconsciously in the nervous system and then (innocently) passed on to others and/or perpetuate pain within ourselves. Violent energy in you and/or another comes from hurt, wounding, pain, and/or loss. Hurt people hurt people. Below is a list of some common expressions of violent energy. This list isn't exhaustive or complete, but it gives you an idea of how to become more aware of violent energy expressions you may encounter in the world.

Types of Abuse	Examples of violent energy manifestations
Physical	Deny physical needs (hydration, rest, food, etc.), sleep deprivation, weapon use, self-harm, throwing, hitting, pushing, slapping, burning, choking, disfiguring.
Emotional	Insulting jokes, silent treatment, ignore feelings, accusations, isolation, humiliation, monitoring, threats, degradation, harming pets, blaming, jealousy.
Social	Use gender myths/roles/bias, destroy property, controls major decisions, threatens family, complete isolation, gas lighting, suicide, denies access to work, eliminates support system, controls finances, child abuse or incest.

Violent energy doesn't help tissues heal. Violent energy perpetuates pain of all kinds—physical, emotional and social. You can prove that to yourself right now: Notice your body and how you feel when you look at the above chart. You likely won't experience pleasant sensations if you really take in the words of that list. Your body chemistry is not in a state that is conducive to health, growth or restoration if it stays in that circuitry for too long.

According to the Oxford dictionary, a victim is "a person harmed, injured or killed as a result of a crime, accident or other event or action." We have all been victims. We have all encountered hurt and harm through and because of the actions of others. The hurt or injury others imposed upon you can be large or small. Whether or not your harm was intentional, the hurt you went through is real and deserves to be restored through compassionate care and appropriate action to heal.

There is a difference between a victim moment and a victim mentality. The victim moment is an injury and needs support to heal. If you don't get the support you need, your nervous system can develop a victim mentality. This is not unlike breaking your leg. You can break a leg, receive good care and things will heal. You will return to walking, running and full function again. Or you can break a leg and not receive good care. Things can heal, but without adequate support, they'll heal a bit wonky and you might develop a limp which can create favoring and cause strain elsewhere later.

There is a difference between a victim moment and a victim mentality.

The victim mentality will physiologically develop if your past victim moments didn't receive adequate care. A victim moment needs compassion. There is injury that deserves supportive kindness. A victim mentality is like someone with a limp who needs retraining to learn how to move again without the limp. Neither deserves to be beaten up for how cruel life was to it. The victim moments within us need compassion for effective healing. The victim mentality within us needs coaching for effective guidance to restore power, full healing and quality of life.

Kristin Neff, PhD, is a researcher that studies compassion. She defines compassion as an energy that is intended to alleviate suffering. Compassion can be directed outward to alleviate suffering, and this is how it is commonly thought of. When energy to reduce suffering is directed inward toward oneself, it's called Self-Compassion. Neff's work also creates a further distinction in two types of compassion: Fierce and tender. Tender compassion is often nurturing, soft and more passive. Tending to a sick child is a good example of this. Fierce compassion is more like a Momma Bear—it's more action oriented. A good example is someone who needs to tap into courage to say no, stand up to an injustice or voice a request to get needs met.

Compassion, both fierce and tender, directed outward or inward, can act as the powerful elixir that encourages more of the empowered roles. Compassion can see that the drama roles are attempts to meet a need. It has access to the space and grace to empathetically recognize that the drama role strategies will never be able to effectively get the needs met. Compassion can ease the discomfort of change as you shift from the dominance of the drama triangles to the capabilities of the empowered roles. Compassion can more effectively recognize the unmet needs in everyone involved and ease the pain from which we all suffer as a result of the perpetual Victim, Rescuer and Persecutor roles.

CHAPTER REFLECTIONS

- ▶ **Consider which relationships** are working well in your life. Reflect on which roles you play in that dynamic and celebrate them.
- ▶ **Reflect** on more challenging and less pleasant relationships in your life and which role you play in them. Remember that you can change roles anytime once you are aware of what's happening within you.
- ▶ **Compassion.** What victim moment occurred in your life that was an injury requiring compassion? How can you make that happen?
- ▶ **Train yourself** to ask empowering questions that promote growth, understanding and positive change. Choose one from the list and make a choice to adopt it this week.

CHAPTER TWELVE

The Mood Meter and Your Four Selves

*"If you're okay with everything,
then everything is okay."*
MICHAEL SINGER

"Where attention goes, neural firing flows, and a synaptic connection grows." Dan Siegel's science-based Mindsight framework is based on this concept and is believed to have originally come from the Tao Te Ching. Your attention is biased and historically programmed to fixate on bad, not good. This concept is related to Hebb's Theory, "Neurons that fire together, wire together." Where your attention goes, energy flows. The attention you pay to the world around and within you will create patterns in your body, breath and mind.

Many people can feel helpless to change difficult circumstances, but the truth is that no one can take from you the ability to change how and where you focus your attention. This shift of your attention will, in turn, change how your nervous system operates. Marc Brackett's Mood Meter is exactly the science-based tool we turn to for support in how to do this.

No one can take from you the ability to change.

Marc Brackett, PhD, is the founder of the Yale Center of Emotional Intelligence and developed the research-based Mood Meter, used in over 3,000 schools across the US and originally created to develop emotional skills in children and adults. We are deeply grateful for this work, as it has proven itself to be profoundly useful.

The Mood Meter has four quadrants:

1. Red is the upper left quadrant: high energy (5-10) and low pleasantness (1-5).
2. Blue is the lower left quadrant: low energy (1-5) and low pleasantness (1-5).
3. Yellow is the upper right quadrant: high energy (5-10) and high pleasantness (5-10).
4. Green is the lower right quadrant: low energy (1-5) and high pleasantness (5-10).

Each color quadrant has words that are used to describe various feelings that match the energy and pleasantness of it. Because there are two 1-10 axes, it allows for more nuance in describing your experience than a traditional "1-10, what's your pain?" type of question.

A copy of the Mood Meter is on page 105. Many people find it helpful to print a copy and put it somewhere they see often. If you'd like to support yourself in developing greater internal awareness, please use this link (https://bit.ly/42UvCwb), print your own copy, and put it somewhere that you see often. Some people have it on the fridge, others on a desk. You can discover what works best for you.

As we played with the Mood Meter, we had some delightful discoveries of some other ways this tool can be used. We'll spend this chapter and the next two, sharing those strategies with you. We are excited to share these practical and attention-building practices in developing greater positive awareness of yourself, your body and your nervous system.

To print your own copy in color, visit **https://bit.ly/42UvCwb**

Adapted from Yale Center for Emotional Intelligence Mood Meter

ENERGY	1	2	3	4	5	6	7	8	9	10
10	ENRAGED	PANICKED	STRESSED	JITTERY	SHOCKED	SURPRISED	UPBEAT	FESTIVE	EXHILARATED	ECSTATIC
9	LIVID	FURIOUS	FRUSTRATED	TENSE	STUNNED	HYPER	CHEERFUL	MOTIVATED	INSPIRED	ELATED
8	FUMING	FRIGHTENED	ANGRY	NERVOUS	RESTLESS	ENERGIZED	LIVELY	ENTHUSIASTIC	OPTIMISTIC	EXCITED
7	ANXIOUS	APPREHENSIVE	WORRIED	IRRITATED	ANNOYED	PLEASED	HAPPY	FOCUSED	PROUD	THRILLED
6	REPULSED	TROUBLED	CONCERNED	UNEASY	PEEVED	PLEASANT	JOYFUL	HOPEFUL	PLAYFUL	BLISSFUL
5	DISGUSTED	GLUM	DISAPPOINTED	DOWN	APATHETIC	AT EASE	EASY GOING	CONTENT	LOVING	FULFILLED
4	PESSIMISTIC	MOROSE	DISCOURAGED	SAD	BORED	CALM	SECURE	SATISFIED	GRATEFUL	TOUCHED
3	ALIENATED	MISERABLE	LONELY	DISHEARTENED	TIRED	RELAXED	CHILL	RESTFUL	BLESSED	BALANCED
2	DESPONDENT	DEPRESSED	SULLEN	EXHAUSTED	FATIGUED	MELLOW	THOUGHTFUL	PEACEFUL	COMFY	CAREFREE
1	DESPAIR	HOPELESS	DESOLATE	SPENT	DRAINED	SLEEPY	COMPLACENT	TRANQUIL	COZY	SERENE

Energy axis (vertical): High (RED) at top, Low (BLUE) at bottom.
Pleasant axis (horizontal): Low (BLUE) at left → High (GREEN) at right. Right side: (YELLOW) top, (GREEN) bottom.

We'd like to invite you to take a moment and look at this Mood Meter. You can think of it like a map that helps orient you to the inner landscape of your emotional nervous system. Start with a high-level perspective or a bird's eye view. Simply notice what you notice. Take it in and get curious about what thoughts come up for you. What questions or curiosities does it bring up? Notice where your eyes are drawn to first and where they go next and then after that. If it's helpful for you, take a moment to jot your observations down in a journal or the margins of this book.

When I (Wilene) first experienced the mood meter through a general observation as you just did, I initially had a delightful experience that was quickly followed by intense wrist pain. Interesting, right? We didn't expect that to happen.

The first place my eyes landed was mostly to the yellow, around the words "lively, enthusiastic, focused, and happy." I said, "I didn't consciously look there—that's just where I landed."

Where your eyes gaze and are drawn to will give you insight into the programming of your nervous system. I was really drawn to the yellow color and words, because I like identifying as that kind of person. When I was focusing on the yellow color and words, I noticed that my body felt happy, my breath was delightfully life giving and I was connected to a sense of lightness and ease.

Then the unexpected occurred.

As I was communicating the happy feelings in my body, an intense left wrist pain emerged. Why would that happen? Well, one perspective is that pain is weird and doesn't follow logical rules. We stayed curious and it took us a few rounds of analysis to figure it out. We used the objective numbers of the Mood Meter and were able to come to a conclusion that makes reasonable sense. We'd like to share that journey with you now.

When an intense pain emerges, it's scary. I suspect that because Wilene's nervous system felt safe in our relational field, other circuits in her system that felt unsafe came out and said, "Hey, we want to feel safe, too!" The pain Wilene was experiencing was interesting, and I encouraged her to stabilize herself by looking at her sensation of wrist pain through a different lens of thinking and to use the numbers of the Mood Meter.

I asked her to focus on the sensation as purely as possible without a story, meaning or interpretation of it. "What is the energy of the raw sensation, 1-10? 1 is low, 10 is high. Neither is good or bad, or right or wrong. Get in touch with the raw sensation and experience it in a new way." When you do something different in the face of pain, you get something different in the face of pain. Wilene was courageously able to do this and determined that the energy was an 8 out of 10.

Next, I asked her to do the same with the raw sensation through the lens of pleasure instead of pain. "What is the level of pleasantness that you are experiencing in the present moment sensation in your wrist?" I encouraged her again to notice the sensation itself, without giving it intellectual interpretation, creating meaning, providing an explanation, or making a story out of it. "Just the sensation—what is the pleasantness of it, 1 is low and 10 is high." This is an incredibly challenging task for a nervous system that is biased to look for pain. Wilene was able to overcome the natural inclination to orient to her painful sensation through a lens of pain 1-10, and instead was able to answer the question by determining that the level of pleasant was a 2 out of 10.

She took a breath and bravely took a chance, brought her attention inward and allowed herself to experience the wrist pain in a different way than she ever had before. When she reported feeling an energy of 8 and a pleasantness of 2, it allowed her to be curious about the pain instead of afraid of it. That curiosity led us to track those numbers on the Mood Meter, and it led us to the word "Frightened."

Wilene didn't realize her wrist pain was communicating that she was frightened. It wasn't until the objective numbers of the Mood Meter that she was able to identify a precise word to describe the sensation of her wrist pain—and that's when clarity emerged between us.

It became clear that there was a subconscious nervous system battle going on between Wilene's most favorite self and her most dreaded self. All of us have "four selves" that relate to the four color quadrants of the Mood Meter:

- Most Favorite Self: the color you enjoy being in the most
- Least Favorite Self: the color you enjoy being in the least
- Most Familiar Self: the color your nervous system is most often in
- Least Familiar Self: the color your nervous system is least often in

Wilene's favorite self is yellow and her least favorite self is red. Sometimes Wilene worries a lot, which she doesn't like, and worry is a red word. Worry also happens to be in close proximity to the word "frightened" on the Mood Meter chart. Wilene said, "I don't want to worry. I just want to live in happy all the time." And that's fair. We all want to be happy. The challenge with that desire is that any experience that isn't happy, we tend to resist. And what we resist, persists. Wilene was resisting the worried and frightened circuits within her. As long as she did that (let's not throw Wilene under the bus here, we ALL do that), those worried and frightened circuits would persist. They were showing up at that moment in the form of wrist pain and were acting like a neurological undertow that kept pulling her away from what she wanted—to be happy.

When it came to Wilene's wrist pain, resisting didn't work. It simply brought about more wrist pain. So, she asked, "What can I do next?" That's a question for all of us: How do we deal with unwanted and unpleasant emotions and experiences? As Wilene said, "Okay, so what's the next step to stop worrying and being frightened?"

The first step is to become aware of the emotional dynamic within you. The second step is to label it. Wilene's wrist pain made her aware of an unconscious emotional dynamic within her body—step one. Step two, she labeled it. She did exactly that through a P&E Pulse Check (you'll learn that later), when she assigned 1-10 numbers of energy and pleasantness to her wrist pain, and then found the word that matched her body experience.

With the numeric Mood Meter awareness, she was able to "Name it to Tame it," and then she was able to connect to her wrist pain in a new way and create new understanding about it. Coincidently (or not), she has not had wrist pain since that exercise, which was several months ago at the time of this writing. Prior to that experience we shared, she would get wrist pain about once a month, and it was always tied to worry. Since that exercise, she's become aware of and relates to her dreaded red self with less fear, which has allowed her to resist the red within her less, and finds herself living more frequently in congruence with her favorite yellow self.

Wilene realized that worry is a *part* of who she is, but it's not the *whole* of who she is. So often we are afraid of the dreaded and less familiar parts of ourselves. This fear in response to these parts of ourselves will get stuck in circuits, ruts and grooves of the nervous system. You might be scared of certain parts of you, so you naturally resist, avoid, ignore, deny, or push them away. Naturally, those parts of you that "aren't acceptable" can fall into the lonely trap of believing they are alone in your system, and this is physiologically terrifying. These disowned parts of you often register in nervous system circuits that are unpleasant and express themselves in the emotional motor programs of less pleasant feelings, as seen in the red and blue quadrants of the mood meter. One way your system can bring your attention and awareness to these disenfranchised parts of you is through screaming out in the form of body pain—just like in Wilene's wrist.

When my red and yellow selves are fighting to be in charge of my system, I will either get constipated or have diarrhea. On a really fun day, I vacillate between both! This is a form of self-sabotage for me, because it often occurs when I am taking strides to advance my professional life to the next level.

When Wilene describes her self-sabotage behaviors, she eats junk food (blue) that makes her sleepy (green) when she wants to focus on her work (which would require yellow).

My most chemically comfortable and familiar self (red) wants my system to stay the same, because it perceives change to be a threat. When I take strides to improve and expand, actions that would create more yellow and green in my life, my red chemistry floods my system, creates panic, worry, and anxiety while incapacitating me from effective, focused work by giving me fecal urgency. Fecal urgency is a phenomenon where I have the urge to run to the bathroom several times an hour, only to discover that I can't actually go because I'm constipated. Fecal urgency in my system is an expression of red physiology. In other words, if my red familiar self is threatened by my yellow self, I will "self-sabotage" as a form of protection to "keep me safe" in the red. That's the battle: My red self is afraid of my yellow self.

I will experience self-sabotage when my most familiar self (red) doesn't want to let my favorite self (yellow) do what it wants to do. They are in a battle, a disagreement, and it shows up for me in the form of not taking professional risks that could yield great reward. If my nervous system is programmed in its default mode network to run red, but I consciously want yellow so I'm going to try to go yellow, I'm always going to be drawn back to red. And then I'm going to beat myself up because I can't stay with the yellow thinking, feeling and behaving. Because my wiring isn't primed, grooved or programmed for yellow, it's programmed for red. I can do this yellow thing for a short period of time, but I'm destined to go back to red, because it's how my nervous system is programmed. So that's how we self-sabotage, because the red is orienting toward surviving not thriving.

There are two other selves that we need to explore here: Our most and least familiar selves. There's a part, or color, of ourselves that we are most familiar with, most chemically comfortable with, and we may or may not like that part of ourselves. What did you see first from a broad stroke perspective when you looked at the Mood Meter? That may be your most familiar self, the place your nervous system is most drawn to pay attention to. Wilene resonates most with her yellow self. That is the energy within her that feels most like home, is in most harmony with her soul and her self energy.

I'd love to say my most familiar place and self is yellow, like Wilene's, but it's not. Through this work, I've discovered that, historically, my most chemically familiar self is red. I wanted to be yellow or green, but my nervous system didn't care what I wanted. It cared about my survival and was chemically committed to being in red to ensure that. That is a great way to suffer—to want something different than what is. I wanted to be living in yellow, but my nervous system was calibrated to red. It was on a different page, and it had a different agenda than myself. I wanted to be thriving, but because of past trauma, my nervous system was organized to focus on surviving and using the fierce fight or flight mode to do so. This is quite normal and common for those with any history of pain, stress or trauma. The nervous system will "get stuck" in a mode of survival and run circuits of red fight/flight mode to stay alive or the blue freeze mode to protect the organism from danger.

It was surprising and uncomfortable for me to admit that red was a place and energy I lived in frequently. No wonder I suffered from adrenal fatigue, IBS and neck pain with headaches for so many years! I'm not saying I liked or consciously enjoyed living the fruits of my red circuits, but I am saying that I didn't know I was addicted to that familiar, subconscious chemical state within myself. Like it or not, the objective truth was that my most familiar self, my most chemically comfortable self, was red.

When I first started exploring this concept, I discovered that my subconscious battle was slightly different than Wilene's. Earlier we demonstrated her subconscious battle emerged in the form of wrist pain. Mine was showing up physically in the form of neck pain and gut problems. Upon deeper discovery, my most familiar self was also creating relationship stress.

Another expression of my most familiar red self was the behavior patterns of rescuing others, hyper achieving, perfectionism, and people pleasing. Ironically, these behaviors were feeding and reinforcing the red circuits within me and contributing to the suffering of being disconnected from my own authentic yellow and/or green self-expression. Society and my upbringing often rewarded yellow expressions. I wanted to be in yellow so I could have my fix for the drug of approval. Unfortunately, I was like a dog chasing its own tail due to the subconscious physiological addiction to the familiar and chemically comfortable red states. My very own behavior patterns trying to get me to yellow, kept me locked up in a nervous system that was becoming ever more familiar with and wired in red.

The subconscious fight I was having was between my most familiar red self, and least familiar green self. My dreaded blue self was the place I'd sink down into when I was tired from fighting, and living in the authentic expression of my favorite yellow self was a long forgotten reality that seemed a distant dream.

The lack of awareness in the struggle between my four selves created a fight in me. I didn't consciously enjoy the fruits of my red circuits (neck pain, relationship tensions, communication frustrations, comfy victim identity), yet it had a strangely familiar subconscious draw to it. The nervous system in me was in a chemical state of addiction to red, and therefore it was familiar and even perceived as safe, despite its troublesome expressions. What a weird and strange juxtaposition to be found in. It was like no matter how hard I tried, I couldn't neurologically let go of that gross, old, beat up red security blanket that was giving me so much safety because of the comfortable familiarity it provided. I took an honest look at the comfort that the familiar fight and flight chemicals gave me from persistent red states and had to decide if it was worth all the financial stress, relationship struggles and health challenges I was experiencing as a result.

The high energy that I was used to resulted in me being deathly afraid of low energy states in my nervous system. I kept myself busy and overwhelmed all the time, could never meditate without wanting to crawl out of my skin and I just couldn't relax. Stillness was terrifying. I didn't feel safe in green or comfortable in yellow. This created a lot of self-sabotage for me, because green and yellow were the very places I needed to go if I wanted to find healing. Health is a naturally occurring event that happens in your biology when you are connected physiologically to more circuits of green and yellow and a dynamic equilibrium of all four colors in balance across the board of your life as a whole.

I decided to stop making red and blue wrong in my life and chose to see them as a part of life, not the whole of life. It enabled me to stop making the thinking error that feelings are permanent. That is a common trap to fall into. When we are flooded in an unpleasant state of the nervous system, we think that the unpleasant color is all there is. When we are hijacked, or flooded, by an Eeyore world of blue, we believe that nothing will change and this is just how it's always going to be. While these feelings are real, valid and true, they are not objective facts that accurately reflect the whole reality of what is possible in one's life experience. If you keep believing the lie that blue or red "is just the way it is," and that nothing can change or be different, you will sadly and certainly stay stuck. The rainbow of life, living in the rapture of being fully alive is exactly that—experiencing *all* the colors. And a Nervous System Ninja can identify, experience and allow all the colors of life to live within and around them confident in their skills to navigate them all—even if it's messy and uncomfortable.

When you are brave enough to tell the truth about what is happening inside of you, that is the moment you begin to set yourself free from the neurobiological chokehold any given color has on you.

Thankfully, I was able to discover more perspectives and skills in navigating the mood meter and my four selves. It's often said that teachers teach what they most need to learn. If I wanted to experience deep joy again, I had to create more space within me to allow all four colors in life to be okay inside of me. Healing and wholeness emerged as I got more comfortable with the scary and unfamiliar green circuits within me.

Once I became aware of my four selves, I could ask myself: How do I want my nervous system to be programmed? I decided that I wanted my most favorite and familiar to both be green. I started wearing more green color, noticing the green experiences and moments of peace and calm in my life. I began identifying as a calmer person. I started using more green words and using them in my daily vocabulary. Low and behold, I started feeling more calm, peaceful and a greater sense of control in my life over time. I decided to stop resisting the red and blue of the world and accepted that they are a necessary part of the wholeness of life.

I also found it helpful to orient to these four colors and four selves by looking at others through that lens. For example, I got curious about how I experienced my father and his four selves. Upon reflection, I discovered that my favorite self of his was yellow, I dreaded his red, my least favorite of his was blue, and least familiar was green. That made so much sense and explained a lot about my own upbringing and how my system was wired—and not in the best kind of ways. Or at least, it wasn't resonating with how I wanted to be living in the world now, today, as an adult.

Looking at the four selves through the lens of another human can allow you greater flexibility in the wiring of your own nervous system and how you look at your own four selves. This will give you more choices in how to apply the concept.

What is your most familiar or chemically comfortable self? What color do you experience most frequently in your life? Is it congruent with how you want to live in the world? Does it align with your values and what's most important to you in the world? If not, would you be willing to tell the truth about that to yourself or another safe person in your world? Are you willing to experience more harmony and resonance in your life at large, even if it means being uncomfortable about some truths within your nervous system?

In order to build new nervous system pathways and better navigate all colors within me, I had to learn how to experience my body sensations. Using the mood meter, I was able to give more unpleasant body sensations a number and a name that accurately described what was happening in any given moment. Once I mastered the ability to "Name it to Tame it," I started to feel more in control of my nervous system, instead of it running the show of my life through my digestive system's fears having me sprint to the bathroom every time I wanted to do something scary and brave—like write this book, for example.

If you want to get better at experiencing a more nimble nervous system, because a flexible nervous system is a resilient nervous system, it requires the ability to move into and out of all of these colors or physiological states. And we cannot change a state if we are not aware of what state we are in. You can recognize that all colors within you are natural, normal and appropriate aspects of being a human. Some are more pleasant than others. When you can connect your body to the mood meter and start labeling the body sensations with numbers and words, you are reshaping your nervous system. Scientific research demonstrated that labeling emotions affected the emotional regulation centers in the brain. Subjects were put into an FMRI and were shown pictures that induced emotion. Subjects were asked what they were feeling and their brain responses were measured and recorded. When subjects labeled a negative emotion, the act of verbalizing the emotion actually deactivated the negative firing in the amygdala (a major processing center for emotions). When subjects labeled a positive emotion, the exact opposite happened. Labeling a positive emotion in the brain reinforces it. Labeling negative emotions makes them weaker in your brain circuits and labeling positive emotions makes them stronger!

Labeling a positive emotion in the brain reinforces it.

A student of mine called hers the Four F's: Familiar, foreign, favorite, and feared. These four selves in you have a color. They might all be different or they might overlap. It will be unique for each of you. Each self has words that can be used to describe them. The more words you have available to describe each favorite self, the more you are able to reshape how that self lives within you. The more you can label the negative around that self, you deactivate its negative charge in your brain. The more you label the positive of how that self lives within you, the more you strengthen its circuits in your brain. Labeling, or verbal observations, allows you to let all four of these selves within you be more comfortable, safe and accepted. As Mr. Rogers so aptly said, "If it's mentionable, it's manageable."

Take some time to reflect and get to know your four selves. Which quadrant in the mood meter is your favorite self? Which quadrant is your most dreaded self? What color is your most familiar self, and what color is your least familiar self? What environments, circumstances or people bring out your least favorite, and which bring out your most favorite? Why do you think each self of yours is the color that it is?

Many people with a history of pain, trauma and prolonged stress are very familiar with the red and blue quadrants in them and less familiar with the yellow and green quadrants in them. Is this you? If so, what can you do to help yourself remember that yellow and green exist in your life, even when you're chemically stuck in red or blue? What steps can you take? How can you set yourself up to remember that all the colors of life are available to you, even if you're not feeling them right now?

Once you have awareness about which self is showing up in any given life event, and you have awareness of how that version of yourself shows up, you have more say in how your nervous system shows up. This allows you a greater sense of control within yourself and gives you more choice in how you want to show up in the events, situations and circumstances of your life.

You may feel out of control in some or a lot of your life. This process will allow you to take some of your power back. It's easier to put out little fires than big fires. A patient of mine was really struggling with this practice, and it was because she went straight into trying to fix her 40-year unhappy marriage. She didn't realize she chose a larger fire than her current skills and resources could handle. Once she started focusing instead on smaller challenges in her life where she had more control, like her neck pain, she started experiencing more success and her confidence grew.

We strongly recommend that you start with small challenges in your life, not big ones. Begin by focusing on a tiny sphere within your life and reclaim authority over what you are capable of controlling—yourself. Start with befriending your dreaded self with its upset about the crumbs on the countertop, not your lifelong challenging relationship with your mother. What are some smaller challenges in your life that you could start with? It might be the annoying dishwasher that keeps breaking, a naughty but ultimately benign puppy behavior or an annoying neighbor mowing their lawn at 9pm. Start with smaller provocations, as opposed to bigger challenges such as your life purpose, stagnant career or major relationship troubles. Set you and your four selves up for success. The more you build a relationship with and get to know your four selves, the more you can widen the circles of your life where you can again feel a sense of control within your body.

CHAPTER REFLECTIONS

▶ **Practice.** Print a copy of the Mood Meter and place it somewhere you see frequently as a reminder to check in with yourself, your nervous system and what feelings you are experiencing.

▶ **Label** your emotional experiences (using the Mood Meter) to regulate, promote understanding and restore a sense of control. Make a choice to believe that all feelings are valid and have purpose in your life.

▶ **Apply.** Check in with your body right now. What are its levels of energy and pleasantness experiences, 1-10? Where does your body exist on the Mood Meter in this moment?

▶ **Become aware** of your favorite, least favorite, most familiar and least familiar selves. Take time to reflect on your emotional patterns and tendencies as they show up in body and mind.

▶ **Choose** which color you want to be your most familiar self. Begin to notice that color in the world more frequently, use the words that belong to that color and appreciate moments of that color in your life with extra attention and celebration.

CHAPTER THIRTEEN

A Deeper Dive into Pulse Checks

*"Until you make the unconscious conscious, it
will rule your life and you will call it Fate."*
CARL JUNG

You previously learned how to orient your awareness and attention to your body and breath with a B&B Pulse Check. We will expand on two other types of pulse checks you can develop and add to your repertoire. We'll apply the concept of pulse checks to the Mood Meter, which serves as a helpful map for our own embodied emotional nervous system. First, we'll do a bit of background to set the stage before you learn the practical skills of these two new pulse checks.

Our bodies are equipped with an intelligent warning system that helps us identify and respond to potential threats and challenges in our lives. Pay attention to this warning system to take better care of yourself and your overall well-being. But you can't just pay any kind of attention. We think it needs to be specifically trained, one that includes curiosity, objectivity and discernment. When you only pay attention to your body and its warning system with your default mode of paying attention, more often than not, you will inadvertently create more trouble for yourself. This is for two main reasons: One is our Negativity Bias for survival, and the other is a Selective Attention on fixing problems that comes from within us and is reinforced by the medical system.

First, let's explore the negativity bias for a moment. When we were cavemen, it was better for our survival to pay attention to a rustling bush and assume it's a lion and not a cute bunny rabbit. We learned this, because our unfortunate caveman cousin learned the hard way when he stuck around to see the cute bunny emerge from the rustling bush, got it wrong, and the lion got him instead. Humans naturally, through brilliant learning mechanisms devoted to survival, pay attention to their bodies only when something is perceived to be wrong, and then the worst case scenario is assumed. We still do this today, because if we didn't, the costs would be high! Like, dead!

This early caveman training created a present day nervous system with a default mode of paying attention mostly to negative sensations in the body. You likely only pay attention to your body when you perceive something is wrong, and then you assume the worst. This is often highly unhelpful and ineffective at creating joy in your life, not because of a character defect, but rather because your nervous system hasn't been trained to pay attention to good stuff in your body. When you don't pay attention to good things, you have not built neural pathways that allow you to experience and sustain good things in your life.

This is why it's hard for patients like John, a 38-year-old IT professional with persistent back pain and longstanding anxiety, to experience a pleasant sensation in his body. He looks at me like I'm crazy when I ask him, "Where does it not hurt in your back?" He has no idea how to answer that and is literally speechless. His attention can't access pleasant circuits inside of him because he hasn't trained his attention to notice positive sensations. All of his attention, when it comes to his back for the previous eight years, has been on what's bad and wrong about it. Attention is like our muscles—if we work them in any given direction, they get better and stronger in the direction where they have a lot of training and repetition.

The second kind of unhelpful attention we practice without knowing it, is our selective attention and fixation on fixing problems. Of course we fixate on fixing! If there's a problem, we want to fix it. If something is wrong in the body, we want to make it better. That's a natural expression of our devotion to wanting to be well.

Sadly, it doesn't work that way.

There's a concept in a wonderful book called, *Super Better*, where we learn more about what *does* work. Jane McGonigal, a researcher, game designer and inventor explains that we don't get better *from* something, we get better *at* something. We don't get better *from* insomnia. We get better *at* sleeping. We don't get better *from* pain. We get better *at* pleasure.

Most of us, including the medical system, are stuck in a trap of trying to *fix* pain, instead of orienting to, focusing on and training our nervous systems to get better *at* pleasure. When we fixate on fixing, it's like we have blinders on that prevent us from having biological access to seeing another way of solving the problem. We just throw more drugs, more surgeries, more diagnoses at the problem to fix it. Even the education of practitioners in the medical system trains the fixation on fixing. You see it every time you go to the doctor and you get asked, "What's your pain, 1-10?" Each time that happens, the nervous system gets reinforced training to get better and better at noticing pain, making it wrong (instead of being a messenger of useful information), followed by the fixation-on-fixing trap. All these things get our nervous systems better, stronger and faster at fixating on the pain and problems.

Now before you go beating yourself up, it's not *you* that is doing the fixing fixation—it's your nervous system. And it's reinforced by the culture, the collective and medical system around you. And probably a whole host of other hidden influences we don't know, recognize or understand. And all of that is okay, because we can change it.

There's a saying, "Do what you always did, get what you always got." If you continue to pay attention to your breath and body with a negativity bias and a fixation on fixing, you will continue to experience pain, anxiety, depression, and unhappiness. It's time to change that, and the rest of this chapter is devoted to teaching you exactly how.

We want you to pay attention to your body and nervous system in a different way so you can create a different experience. You are going to pay attention to your system with a new lens of objectivity. When you do something different, you get something different. Next, you will explore and expand your Pulse Check skills with two new practices: A Three Word Check-In and a P&E Pulse Check.

Three Word Check-In

A Three Word Check-In is a form of labeling or making a verbal observation of your own nervous system. It's simply doing an honest inventory of your own nervous system at any given moment, and then describing your experience with three words. Remember, scientific studies prove that labeling "negative" emotions, or less pleasant words in the blue and red Mood Meter quadrants, deactivates their charge in your amygdala. And labeling positive emotions, or more pleasant words in the yellow and green Mood Meter quadrants, does the opposite! Labeling positive emotions reinforces and strengthens their potency in your nervous system. Don't be fooled by the simplicity of naming three words.

Three Word Check-Ins, like any pulse check, is best done with regular frequency and consistency. You can do them when you're in a "good place" or a "bad place." Either way will benefit and support you toward greater health. You can use words from the Mood Meter, or you can use any words that suit you. Some people enjoy getting really creative; they make up words, create sounds or just blurt out whatever resonates with their current moment experience.

Happy, peaceful and loving
Angry, drained and morose
Anxious, disappointed and scared
Playful, secure and ecstatic

The sky's the limit for you—fly free!

I (Renée) found that repeating the Three Word Check-In during a high period of stress was particularly regulating. I was traveling to Santa Barbara on what should have been a two-hour plane trip, which ended up taking a total of 15 hours. At one point, while on hold with customer service during my third canceled flight, I started doing lightning repeat rounds of Three Word Check-Ins: Fury, hateful, rage. Spinning, glad, mad. Hateful, wondering, curious. Frustrating, tense, upset. Calming, breath, feet. Exhale, settling, mad. Sad, scared, hopeful. Okay, optimistic, scared. Worried, concerned, breath. Grounding, settling, yellow. Sunshine, outside, window. Breathing, calmer, peace.

You can use any word, sound, image—whatever you want to name your present moment experience. There's no wrong way to do a Three Word Check-In. As you allow yourself to name whatever is true and real for you, you are practicing self-acceptance, which is a really healthy habit to engage with. As I was settling my nervous system through a repeated Three Word Check-In, I noticed my attention was naturally and organically going back to a B&B Pulse Check. My attention was drawn toward my feet. This shift from my frustration to my feet was extremely supportive in helping me ground myself during a stressful situation.

I kept going around and around the world of the Mood Meter, giving myself permission to feel every single feeling, but not to dwell on any given experience. Repeated Three Word Check-Ins at a lightning pace prohibited me from staying anywhere too long, and giving my inner critic voice the time, space and opportunity to make it wrong. As I kept repeating, I watched the words transform from stress to peace as my state transformed. I witnessed my own state transform as the words shifted around, not getting stuck in any one place. It almost seemed like an alchemical process of transformation from extreme fear, panic and rage, into a more regulated state of being grounded, calm and peaceful. I had a good 15-hour trip in the end, learned a lot and even enjoyed the extra time with my sister.

The added bonus of doing Three Word Check-Ins is also worth mentioning. We do these in professional meetings and group trainings. Clinically, we have seen people grow in their self-awareness, emotional skills, connection to themselves, and develop healthier boundaries. When you practice this skill with others, it trains your ability to allow others to be separate in their own experience, while you stay centered in your own circle of experience. When you witness someone in their experience, without needing to change, fix or rescue them, you are empowering both yourself and the other. By allowing the experience to be what it is, you are lessening the roles of Victim and Rescuer in the social dynamics of your collective nervous systems.

Lastly, it's also a practice for greater allowance of diverse and paradoxical experiences to occur in a single moment. For example, people will often have mixed words in a Three Word Check-In: Hopeful, exhausted, curious. This benefits you because it trains your attention to not get vigilantly fixated on any one given emotion. It's like a river of meditation, and you're standing at the edge watching all your emotions go by without too much attention to any one particular feeling. This will bring you greater peace and a richer, more full experience of life and all its vibrant colors.

P&E Pulse Check

The next pulse check skill you'll learn is a P&E Pulse Check: Pleasantness and Energy. This allows you to create more awareness of and connection to the emotions in your body. This is a potent skill to improve your navigation skills of your emotional motor programs. You are going to take an objective, numerical reading of your own nervous system and gather data on two measurements: Pleasant and Energy. Some people really do well with a buddy system or having a check-in confidante. It provides an opportunity to be seen and witnessed. It can allow potential for receiving support by remembering you're not alone and can give accountability for you to continue the development of this skill. Consider if it would be helpful for you to include this as a part of your training. I've had people include it in their family dinners, partnership bonding or parent-child connections. Wilene and I do them frequently at the start of our meetings or throughout whenever we need to restore a sense of grounding and connection.

To do a P&E Pulse Check, all you need to do is connect your awareness to any kind of body sensation. You could decide to connect to something pleasant, neutral or unpleasant. Once you decide what you want to label (which will support greater regulation connected to that sensation), you will give that sensation a number 1-10 as you experience it in energy (or arousal, nervous system level of excitation), and then give that same sensation another number 1-10 in pleasantness. Then you find the corresponding word on the Mood Meter that goes with those numbers. This will then enable you to label your body sensation with a feeling.

Let's start with the easier one. Become aware of your breath and body. Choose any sensation (could be anything including but not limited to tightness, achy, breathless, tension, fuzzy, lightheaded, dizzy, calm, open, light, heavy, queasy, shaky, cramped, thick, tender, etc.) that catches your awareness or interest, and then give it a number. What is the energy, 1-10 (1 is low, 10 is high)? After you have assigned a 1-10 number of energy to that sensation, then assign an objective number to the pleasantness of it, (1 is low, 10 is high.) Now you have two numbers, the first for energy and the second for pleasantness.

Some people may experience difficulty in connecting with pleasant body sensations, particularly if they have had a longstanding history of pain, trauma and/or dissociation. There is a special troubleshooting guide at the end of the chapter to address that, and you may find value in skipping ahead to read that first if you can relate to the difficulty of feeling pleasant sensations in the body.

For part two of your P&E Pulse Check, please reference the Mood Meter on page 105 as needed.

Now that you have your energy number, find the corresponding row on the left-hand side of the chart (where the vertical numbers measure energy). Then find your pleasantness number (on the bottom of the chart where the horizontal numbers measure pleasantness) and find the corresponding vertical column.

There will be a single square where your two numbers intersect. For example, a 6 pleasant and 4 energy is located in the box that says "calm." An 8 energy and 2 pleasant will be "frightened." Find the word that your numbers have mapped you to. Does that word resonate with your current body sensation? If not, look around to see which word(s) in the vicinity might describe your sensation more accurately.

Take a breath and ask yourself, is it okay to feel that way? Yes or no is totally okay. Did you know you were feeling that way? And what do you want to do with that information? Now that you can connect language to your body sensation, you have more room to decide your next course of action. You now have a choice, as opposed to being caught in a reactionary loop of your subconscious programming. There is more freedom, choice and power available to you when you widen the gap between your response to any given sensation or stimulus in your nervous system. That is what you're training with this P&E Pulse Check. You are widening the gap between stimulus and response. This creates greater awareness of where you are and what's going on inside of you, similar to 3D Perspective Taking.

The first and most important thing to understand when you do a P&E Pulse Check, is to not make any of it wrong. The second key point is to set appropriate expectations. Third, the most effective time to do pulse checks is actually when you have the least desire to do them. If you can find motivation to overcome this natural resistance, it will serve you well.

Let's explore each of these three key points a bit further. The first key is to not make any of your experience wrong. Pleasant and unpleasant, highs and lows are natural expressions of the nervous system. These ups and downs are indicators that we are in alignment with the natural order of the Universal rhythm. We can't sleep, eat or heal without low energy. We can't exercise, have sex or face challenges without high energy. The tendency to judge certain experiences as "wrong" will lead to suffering. When assessing pleasantness, it's important for you not to label any experience as "wrong." Just like your energy levels, pleasantness naturally goes up and down. It's an appropriate expression for your nervous system to have highs and lows. It's not wrong, nor is it bad.

There is nothing wrong with you, and there is nothing wrong about you. Your whole system is working together perfectly. No matter where you are, it is perfectly okay. If you stop making you, your nervous system and your experience wrong, your human system wouldn't have to go into fight, flight or freeze to protect you from being wrong, bad, filled with shame, and all the fear, disconnection and isolation that comes with that trap. Once you stop making your experience wrong, your nervous system can retire from having to scratch and claw its way back to being right or good enough. Not making your body and experience wrong will stop making you sick from the body's unending fight against you making it wrong.

There is nothing wrong with you, and there is nothing wrong about you.

When we make things wrong or bad, the nervous system cannot differentiate an experience from itself. So ultimately, when we make things, sensations, other people, or experiences in our system wrong or bad, we make ourselves wrong or bad. This is the physiological origin of shame and the birthplace of your sucky stuck staying stuck. Don't do it. Do P&E Pulse Checks instead.

The second key to a successful P&E pulse check experience is to be aware of your expectations: Set yourself up for success by having realistic, appropriate expectations.

P&E Pulse Checks can be particularly challenging for you if you are used to having pain in your body or you're not accustomed to paying attention to your body. When you begin orienting to your body, particularly pleasant sensations, it can feel as difficult as lifting a 100-pound dead weight barbell after being hospitalized for months. You're not used to paying attention to pleasant, so the circuits in your system are not strong. What's the solution? Start with a very low bar and give yourself lots of encouragement and cheerleading for taking on the courageous work that will improve your life.

The final key ingredient with pulse checks is to do them when you don't want to. How frequently have you experienced the desire to avoid the exact action that would lead to an improvement in your well-being? Do you ever feel like not exercising, but you want the feel-good chemicals that come with exercise? It's a conundrum. You want the effect without doing the uncomfortable action that will create the effect you want. You won't get the effect without taking the action that you don't want to take. The struggle is real. As Brené Brown says, "Embracing the suck is really about embracing uncertainty, risk, and emotional exposure. It's choosing courage, even when it's hard and uncomfortable."

The best way to get the most out of pulse checks is to do them as often as you can. P&E Pulse Checks can be a lot easier when you're feeling more good than bad. You may remember to do pulse checks throughout the day or you may want to set reminders for yourself. And if you stay with the practice of developing your curious self-awareness through pulse checks, you'll likely find yourself inspired and immersed in new moments that will generate and create new circuits within your own nervous system. These breakthrough moments will fuel a momentum within you to keep up the pulse check practice.

With more reps, time and continued skill building, you will enable yourself to feel more in control of your nervous system, your health and your life again. It's our experience, that with time and continued practice of developing deeper self-awareness through pulse checks, *if you stick with the practice,* you'll see that P&E Pulse Checks are the best thing on earth to help you orient to where you are on the Mood Meter map, which also serves as a nervous system map to your own life experience. If you like, want or need a sense of control in your life, pulse checks will help get you there.

It's okay to be okay, and it's okay not to be okay. Doing P&E Pulse Checks with objective curiosity will train your system to be okay with whatever is happening. The more you train, the more your self-acceptance will sink down into deeper and deeper layers of your own nervous system.

In the beginning, it works for many to start with doing some kind of pulse check 1-3 times a day and ultimately build up to 2-3 times per hour. It doesn't matter which type of pulse check you do; you are developing the habit of frequently checking in with your own system. If you have a trauma history, Eric Gentry, PhD Master Traumatologist, recommends building up to 200 times per day of intentionally relaxing the muscles in your body, which roughly works out to every 3-5 minutes throughout your day. Picture my eyes rolling backward along with you when I say this: Yes, you heard it right—200 times! Don't worry, it took me (Renée) about six years to build up to that much frequency. And honestly, most days I have no idea if I come anywhere near 200. I'm a big fan of realistic expectations and beginning with a low bar.

As you get your reps in with pulse checks, it's worth spending time in curious reflection and/or writing in a journal. What people, environments, situations, or circumstances elicit what colors in you? Look for trends and patterns. Does your nervous system always go red when that certain boss walks into the office? Do you notice blue every time Sunday rolls around and you need to face the work week ahead? Is there one person that you know always evokes a yellow response in you? Is there a certain activity you do that creates green within you?

What colors did you grow up in? Was there a lot of yelling and higher energy around? Or was it more the opposite, where everyone suppressed everything and only low energy green and blue were allowed? What did your nervous system learn growing up was okay and not okay? How does that impact your present relationships and environments? What colors show up in your relationships today? Which colors are you okay with in relationships, and which colors are you not okay with? How, if at all, does that relate to what your nervous system is okay and not okay with in present experiences?

Have you ever said the words, "I don't like conflict"? Perhaps your nervous system learned growing up that conflict was red and you didn't like it. It didn't feel safe to your nervous system, so now, naturally as an adult, you make red wrong because it's neurologically uncomfortable. Yet somehow you keep finding red energies (or they keep finding you) in unpleasant work or home situations. Why does that happen? Because on some level your nervous system resists red, and what we resist, persists.

As you develop more pattern recognition of how your nervous system shows up in different contexts of your life, you have more awareness of cause and effect. This awareness gives you the power and freedom to choose what, how and where you want to live your life. The biological roots of your nervous system create the fruits of your life.

As we've already explored, we all have a negativity bias and fixation on fixing pain. These are not character flaws. They are natural expressions of our social conditioning and human evolution. That being said, these natural biases can make orienting to pleasantness within your body a real challenge. You can likely expect some degree of difficulty finding a number 1-10 of how pleasant something within you is, especially if you are used to experiencing a lot of pain.

Troubleshooting Pain in a P&E Pulse Check

If you are used to having a lot of pain in your mind or body and not used to experiencing pleasure, fear not. It can change. Here's what you can do:

If you struggle with connecting to a sensation and assigning it a pleasantness level of 1-10, you can reverse your painful lens of orientation to a pleasant one by subtracting your pain level from 10. If your pain level is extremely high, it's important to seek quality support, connection, resourcing, and care. When feeling outside of your window of tolerance, you can force yourself to orient to something in your environment that is either neutral or pleasant to break free from the neurological story and physiological "prison." There is nothing wrong with struggling to assess pleasantness, and with time and practice, it will become easier.

If it is totally and utterly impossible for you to connect to a sensation and identify it as 1-10 pleasant, not to worry. All is not lost for you. You just simply need to do an extra step. Find the sensation in your body that has grabbed your attention by the throat—the sensation that has you gripped so tightly that you simply cannot focus on anything else. That's not wrong, it happens to us all. You're okay, and it's okay. Follow this simple math formula to start to find your way out.

Identify that gripping sensation with painful lens. 1-10, what is the pain? Let's say it's really high, like an 8 out of 10. No problem (even though it totally feels that way) you need to do is subtract 8 from 10, which gives you a 2. So, now you've reversed your painful lens of orientation to a pleasant lens of orientation. Instead of an 8/10 pain, you have 2/10 pleasant. Not high, but it's a number, and it will help you break from the neurological story and its resulting physiological prison cell that you are stuck in.

Any type of grounding exercise can be supportive at orienting you toward more neutral (and maybe even eventually pleasant!) sensations within your body.

You'll get more and more okay with whatever is emerging in your nervous system. You will become more and more okay with letting things be as they are. And you will gradually have more and more tolerance (you can even develop appreciation, with enough time and compassion) for whatever colors, numbers, experiences, and words that happen to describe feelings within you. It will all be okay again.

CHAPTER REFLECTIONS

- ▶ **Recognize** that your nervous system tends to focus on negative sensations due to an ancient survival mechanism. Where do you perceive the worst-case scenarios even in non-threatening situations? Acknowledge this tendency without judgment.
- ▶ **Shift your attention** from problem toward solution. What is it that you want to get "better from," and what can you get "better at" instead?
- ▶ **Think about pulse checks** like building a tunnel. Even if you feel nothing and don't see the value, there is still a benefit to be had. Consider the movie *Shawshank Redemption* — it took Andy Dufraine years to dig his tunnel out of jail, but his persistence eventually set him free.
- ▶ **Remember: If you're okay with everything, then everything is okay.** That includes not being okay. It is okay for you to not be okay. And it's okay to be okay.

CHAPTER FOURTEEN

Navigating the Colors of Your Nervous System

*"Perception is not always reality. And reality
is not always the same as what we perceive.
Because human senses can be wrong, and
humans can give different interpretations of what
they see, hear, taste and feel. That is why we
cannot rely completely on one thought. Human
conclusions tend to be relative and uncertain.
He is always at a distance from the truth."*

TITON RAHMAWAN

In a previous chapter, we talked about 3D Perspective Taking as a tool to gather information about any pain you are experiencing. As a reminder, those three dimensions are physical, emotional and social. Next, you are going to learn a new exercise called Around the World Storytelling. We named it Around the World Storytelling because it is an exercise that allows you to explore any given object or circumstance through four different colors on the mood meter. This will allow you to have four perceptions of any given thing, event or experience, instead of just being trapped in one perception of the world around and within you. This enables you to change your pain cycle and gives you another avenue in which you can complete any potential incomplete stress cycles stuck within your nervous system.

In the last two chapters, you explored and discovered different ways you can use the Mood Meter to learn more about your nervous system. Around the World Storytelling will allow you to apply your newfound knowledge into a practical technique that will immediately settle your nervous system, expand your perspectives and make you feel better.

We have mentioned the term "Nervous System Ninja" a few times, and we'd like to clearly define what it means. A Nervous System Ninja is someone who has access to confidence in the "UNs of Life": The Unknown, the Unwanted and the Unexpected. In other words, you can remain connected to a sense of confidence in your ability to cope with life's uncertainties. In regards to this chapter, a Nervous System Ninja can identify when they're in any specific color and then have the ability to shift colors to one that is more favorable or congruent with the experience of their desired outcome.

The pain points in our life (physical, emotional and/or social) can trap us (our nervous system) in one or two of the Mood Meter colors. That single color trap can trick us into thinking that's all there is, and that's the way it will always be. For example, someone with persistent back pain experiences their back problems through a very blue state (depressed, hopeless and pessimistic). And then sure enough, the movement patterns of the back muscles continue to perform in a very painful, blue kind of way, creating an unfortunate self-fulfilling prophecy. Another person with nagging money issues might live with a nervous system historically stuck in a program of red (frustration, anxiety and stressed), so they are caught in the trap of constant worry and an empty bank account.

What pain points in your life are you (and/or your nervous system) caught up in? List them out and take an honest inventory of the areas in your life that are unsatisfying to you. Then assign a color to each struggle or pain point in your life. Reference the Mood Meter as needed.

Embark on a journey with us to discover the boundless spectrum of colors, unveiling countless perspectives that reveal the vibrant tapestry of your world and everything it encompasses.

Each of your pain points can live in more than the one color that you assigned to them. We invite you to consider this an exploration or an adventure that allows you to expand your perspectives, and you will grow the skills of being flexible in your nervous system. This is to your advantage because problems in your life most often biologically drive your nervous system into rigidity, which is not helpful and will keep you stuck. You will literally change every problem and pain point in your life when you learn and apply this skill to your challenges. Are you open to tapping into your Inner Creator and cultivating a sense of inspiration and delight within you? Are you willing to recognize your own ability to create new opportunities and experiences for yourself?

Around the World Storytelling

Stand up in a room. If you can't stand for whatever reason, no problem, just visual choose four distinct spots on a wall or floor around you. If you can stand, go ahead and do so, and create four imaginary boxes on the floor in front of you, like a giant Mood Meter Twister Board is lying on the floor before you. Next, choose a neutral object in the room or space around you. For example, it might be a mouse pad, a plant or a piece of furniture. Once you have selected your object, you can place it in front of you, or stand in front of it. Choose a color from your imaginary Mood Meter Twister board (blue, red, green, yellow) and stand in it. Whichever color you are drawn to first is fine. Follow whatever impulse or instinct you have. Again, if you can't stand, just focus your visual attention on that color as you imagine it on the wall in front of you.

Once you step into that square, it's as if you are becoming one with that color. You are in control and in charge of how deeply (or not) you want to experience that color. Holding the Mood Meter in your hand, look over the emotions on it and choose a few of the words from the color you are standing in. Feel the words as they live in your body, experience them in your mind and stay curious about how your nervous system shows up in that color. Remember that you can leave the color at any time. You are not trapped or powerless and there is likely nothing objectively or physically dangerous about standing in the room that you are in.

Next, describe your chosen object as you see it from that color. Make up a story about that object: How do you experience it? What do you think about it? What posture does it create in you? How does it make you breathe? What does it make you want to do? What body impulse do you notice? Say your story out loud, describe what that object is for you to hear, and then notice what meaning you make of it from this color of your physiology.

Then, complete and close with that color, story and perspective. Literally shake your body, step out of that color, take a breath, and *notice that you can leave it behind.*

Choose the next color and repeat the process.

Once you've done that for all four colors, notice that the object is neutral, yet your experience, story and meaning about it have four different narratives. And then notice that those four different narratives live in four different ways in your mind and body and affect your thinking and behaving in four different ways. Take some time here to journal any discoveries, insights or aha moments you might have.

Now that you have the basics of Around the World Storytelling down, you're going to apply that to a slightly more challenging experience. Don't start with the biggest pain point in your life, as tempting as that can be. Start with a mild to moderate challenge in your world, perhaps a slight annoyance in your life, such as leaves blowing all over your front lawn after you just raked or the work of feeding your dogs if you're not feeling it. Anything that evokes a level of resistance or difficulty in you, but not so much that it overwhelms you with big emotions or stress.

Let's use my (Wilene) example of feeding my dogs and the occasional resistance I have around that.

- From standing in red, the perspective is, "There are six of them! It's so many and the responsibility is sometimes overwhelming."
- Shift into blue, and the story becomes, "This is exhausting, I don't want to, I wish somebody else would do this, but it's just me, lonely me."

- My green story is that, "I am grateful for them and feel secure with their presence. Overall, feeding five dogs can be a lot, but we have a program, and it can be a very calm time. It's nice to experience the calm with them."
- Step into yellow and the narrative becomes, "I'm happy to have them, I smile when I see them, they bring joy to my life, they're all rescue and they've rescued me."

It's nice to have choice in how we see things. This exercise trains your nervous system to be able to shift its physiology between the four different perspectives you can have as you travel around the Mood Meter World.

When you do this exercise, you are developing flexibility in your Perspective Taking of the world. Each color and perspective is real, true, valid, and fair. None of them is bad or wrong; they are simply different, and each perspective is a natural, biological occurrence of the physiology. All four perspectives of feeding the dogs are valid. As you practice moving your body in and around the four colors, naming them, and moving between them, you are literally building the circuits of flexibility that allow you to have more awareness and choice of the perspectives you have of objects, people, situations, and circumstances of your life.

You can do Around the World Storytelling with anything. Start with neutral objects until you get the hang of switching colors in your Perspective Taking. Build up to events, people or circumstances that have more meaning to you. It might be fun to start with something you really love. You can practice Around the World Storytelling with people in your life (past or present), times or seasons in your life, events that have occurred, current or future events—get creative! When developing these skills from simple to more complex and challenging, It can sometimes be helpful to write down what you want to do on a piece of paper. For example, my father has passed away, but I can use a photo of him. Or I can put a dollar bill in front of me to discover my around the world stories and four perspectives around money. You can write your pain point down on a piece of paper and place it before you.

Notice how your body responds, go to that color and then go around the world. The expansiveness of your imagination and creativity is the only limit with this practice.

As you build the capacities and skills within you, you can build up to the bigger pain points in your life that you listed earlier. Those are often the most challenging, yet also the most important to do, because they tend to have the deepest grooves in your nervous system and can often be the hardest to change. That's why we recommend starting with easy stuff first. If you go straight to the hardest pain point in your life, you may not have the circuits built up in your nervous system yet. You may struggle or fail and think the exercise doesn't work. It's a game changer. Don't deprive yourself of the goodness by starting out with too much, too soon.

Nervous systems want and need fluidity, diversity and change. Many folks with a history of trauma, persistent pain or stress have nervous system pathways that are deeply embedded grooves in the red and blue lanes of the Mood Meter—especially 1-2 pleasant levels. Practicing Around the World Storytelling will support you to start having more yellow and green experiences in your body, mind and life.

One way to do that is to shorten the distance between tears and laughter. This is a great way to enhance flexibility of your nervous system and become more resilient from the inevitable tragedies, losses and difficulties in life.

When my healthy, 47-year-old mother suddenly and unexpectedly died, it was very traumatic. There was an overwhelming amount of shock, tears and trauma in the chemicals of my nervous system and very little chemical activity of laughter, joy and happiness in that set of circuits within me for quite a long time. All of this is normal, natural and makes perfect sense given the context that was happening at the time.

When my healthy, 82-year-old father also died unexpectedly from COVID in 2021, I was surprised at how non-traumatic his passing was. Please don't get me wrong. I experienced high and intense volumes of sadness, grief, fear, loss, and bereavement. Yet at the same time, none of those waves "took me out" because I felt very capable to ride those intense waves. I was grateful and aware of all the support, love and safety around that helped me.

I had a long distance between tears and laughter with my mom's death and suffered a lot for a long time. I had a short distance between tears and laughter with my dad's death and didn't suffer as much. I felt a lot of grief, sadness and loss, but was present to it, felt it purely and fully. The lack of resisting it allowed it to move through me, and spontaneous laughter would sprinkle the grief process to lighten the load, leaving me less traumatized by the whole thing.

It's surprising to me that I can share I didn't experience trauma with my dad's death, because I felt supported, loved and connected through the whole thing (neighbors, sisters, family, friends). It also helped that I was 43 years old, and I had more nervous system regulation skills than I did as an 11-year-old! The distance between tears and laughter with my dad's death was very short. Laughter was the chemical buffer to balance out the heaviness of our loss, and it's a biologically remarkable indicator of a human system's natural resilience.

I had trauma living inside of me from my mom's death for over 30 years. It affected and compromised my well-being in every way: Physical and mental health challenges, relationship struggles with insecure attachment and unhealthy codependency. The distance between tears and laughter with my mom's death was very long. I know this because I would drown in sadness every time I was reminded of my mom not being here with me when I wanted her to be—to watch her kids and grandkids grow up, to grow old with her husband, etc.

When I think of her now and feel that overwhelming sadness, I recall a story about six-fingered Mary. On the rough draft image of my mom's tombstone there is Mother Mary and as we looked closely at Mary holding the baby Jesus, we noticed the artist had drawn Mary with six fingers on her right hand! When I think of six-fingered Mary, it bridges the gap from tears to laughter. I can now smile instead of feeling consumed by sadness. I can breathe easier instead of feeling constricted by a heavy chest that felt suffocated for so long by my stuck tears. I brought some yellow to the blue when I dug around in my memory bank to recall six-fingered Mary.

You can balance out the stories of your past. Think about the worst thing(s) that ever happened in your life. Dig through the recesses of your brain and its memories. What color(s) are those memories? Then see if you can find the first time you remember laughing after that bad event(s) occurred. My mom's death, prior to recalling six-fingered Mary, lived in me like I was drowning in an ocean of blue sadness. When I first challenged myself with this exercise, it took me several days to recall the first time I remembered a moment of laughter. I had 30 years of reps and practice with sadness when it came to anything related to my mom, so of course it was a challenge to find some yellow in all that blue! It might be awkward, foreign or unfamiliar for you to find some laughter, joy, fun, or play around the times of your own difficulties, but it's worth doing. That's the cool thing about your brain: If you ask it a question, it will look for an answer. That's why it's good to ask thoughtful, helpful and supportive questions that get you somewhere better, as opposed to common inner critic questions like, "Why am I so stupid?"

We think that love is often a choice, as opposed to a warm and mushy feeling. You can choose to accept that all the colors in life are normal, natural and necessary. We're not saying you have to like or want less pleasant aspects of life, but we do encourage you to consider that the fullness of nature includes all colors. If you can choose to accept that fact, you will be happier. The more you reject and/or tolerate the less pleasant colors of life, the less joyful you will be. It doesn't always feel good to accept and love yourself with all your colors. Love doesn't always feel good; sometimes it's a choice you have to make to accept all colors within you, even if you don't like or want it. The fullness of *your* nature includes all colors, and the more you can recognize and guide yourself and your nervous system, through all the colors with awareness and choice—the more fluidly you will move through life, and the less pain you'll have in any given dimension of your being—physical, emotional or social.

We are social creatures, wired for connection. Healing doesn't happen in a change to vacuum. You can do Around the World Storytelling by yourself to train and develop the flexibility of your nimble nervous system. And if you want to take your healing to a level beyond what you believed possible, let yourself be witnessed in doing the exercise. Maybe start with a pet, because they definitely won't judge you and they'll love you in all the colors. Then, step into a brave act of power, and ask a safe person if they will witness you do some Around the World Storytelling. It has a powerful way of connecting you to the life experience of another human being.

We all have all the colors, and when we allow them, and allow them to be empathically witnessed by another (and not made wrong, not critically condemned or judged), it builds a powerful connection that promotes healing on levels that runs deeper than our conscious brain can really comprehend, but knows and believes it's true. I don't understand how my skin heals after I cut it, but I trust that process. It's the same with humans. We can hurt one another, and we can heal one another. Letting yourself be witnessed by another can heal you on levels that run deeper than you understand. Thank goodness for Einstein, who said that imagination is more important than understanding. No matter what color you may be stuck in, the most important thing is to imagine that the other colors still exist, even if you're not feeling connected to them yet.

Often a nervous system will get locked up in a color, and the proverbial horse blinder effect will create a loss of access to other colors; because of that people begin to believe "that's just the way it is." Around the World Storytelling helps you change your physiology, so that you can see anything from four different perspectives. And each of them is valid, fair and true, *from that perspective.*

When you hear the word money, what is the first color your nervous system in? First color that pops up. When Wilene was asked, she said red because money can be frustrating or rather the flow of money can be frustrating when it's not flowing the way she desires it to come in. Then I watched a lightbulb go off and I asked her what that moment was. She said, "I just realized I could easily shift that red to a green, having peace around money and be in gratitude." It was a moment of deeper clarity for us both that we can all create choice in how we see things in our lives.

This is why affirmations don't work for so many people. As an example, Wilene would use a lot of positive affirmations when it came to money, yet continued to feel frustrated that they weren't working. Until she did the Around the World Storytelling, she didn't realize when it comes to money, her nervous system was stuck in a red mode. She realized this when she experienced back pain during the exercise when she wanted to shift her money perception from red to green.

What color are you in when you see that problem in your life? What color do you want to be in? Who can change that? A nimble Nervous System Ninja can identify what color their nervous system is in, and then shift into a different state, if needed, to align their physiology in a way that may be more congruent with the desired outcomes.

You, as a Nervous System Ninja, can also discover deeper underground belief systems that may be lurking in your operating system through a deeper investigation of how your body shows up in the four colors of the Mood Meter. An interesting exercise to do: Go back to your imaginary four colors on the floor. Stand in one color at a time, get as present in body and mind as you can to that color and then finish each sentence stem:

I am: ____

The world is: ____

You are: ____

My problem is: ____

This is another eye-opening exercise for many; it reveals beliefs about yourself, the world, how you see others, and the challenges in your life. I am a very loving person in green, a happy person in yellow, a complete a**hole in red, and a miserable, lonely loser in blue. The world is "a fun place to be" when I stand in yellow, "crappy and super uncomfortable" when I stand in red, "beautiful and evokes awe" when I stand in green, and "a miserable pit of despairing hell" when I stand in blue. The color your physiology is in literally drives how you see everything. Whichever most familiar self you have will greatly experience the beliefs you have about everything in your life.

What if you knew, you could prime the pump of your nervous system? You can prepare your nervous system for future events through a three-step process. This involves becoming aware of how you think about and anticipate future events by using the colors and setting a different expectation within your nervous system. The First Step for you to do this is to create awareness of your neural expectancy for future outcomes by asking yourself, "What am I expecting in this situation, with this person? What color is that neural expectation?"

For example, many people don't like going to the dentist. Their nervous system is primed for and expecting red: Tension, stressed, worried, apprehensive, fearful, etc. And then how often does priming of the neurological pump become a self-fulfilling prophecy? We would venture to say that is likely a familiar experience that many could relate to.

The Second Step to changing your neural expectancy is to expand your curiosity and imagination around what is possible with the future event, person or circumstance. What other colors could be possible as you engage with this anticipated future event, circumstance or person? As you prepare to go to the dentist, could you imagine noticing the kind way that the receptionist smiles to greet you, and then registering that feeling of gratitude in your body? That might be a nice welcome, yellow chemical break from the red pool of anxiety and worry. Or could you possibly imagine the future moment where you recognize that you survived the dentist? You can imagine seeing yourself walk out of the office and connecting to the felt sense of more yellow sensations in your body. This will often lead you straight into the Third Step where you can smile, feel proud of yourself and you celebrate (I literally say to myself, "Way to go, Renée!") for doing something you didn't want to do because you value having a healthy set of teeth and gums.

The Third Step is to celebrate yourself, and all of the color possibilities of your future, by saying "Way to go, _______ (insert name here). You just jiggled your nervous system loose from the monochromatic chains of its past neural expectancy! When you start looking for diversity of color in future possibilities, you will break yourself free from the painful chains of your past experiences.

The above three steps can influence, shape and change your future experiences. Sometimes the change in your outcome can be fast; Emilia's elbow pain resolved within a few weeks after her discovery and application of these steps. Other times, it can take longer than you think or want. Oftentimes, this can depend on how deep the trenches are in your nervous system; in other words, how long and deep has this negative expectancy been plaguing you. Emilia had pain for three months, and it resolved within weeks using this technique. For me (Renée), I had dental anxiety and avoidance for seven years after a traumatizing experience, and it took me two years to be able to change my predicted and actual experience of the dentist from red to yellow and green.

Around the World Storytelling can be like an infinity loop that never ends. As long as you keep doing reps and take breaks when you need to, you will build up flexibility and expand possibilities of perspective in your nervous system that you could have never imagined before. Imagine standing in the middle of an infinity loop; your body and this moment of *now* are at the intersection point between the two loops. There is an infinite number of possibilities for you. You can do Around the World Storytelling of your past, present and future. You have learned the skills to change the color of your physiology in your *now*, and as you do that, you send ripples out into the infinity loops of your present and past, opening an infinite number of doors for new possibilities in your life.

CHAPTER REFLECTIONS

▶ **Balance tears and laughter.** Recall the first moment you remember humor or laughter after a difficult event. Think about, savor and share this memory to provide a chemical buffer against being drowned by trauma and stress circuits within you.

▶ **Four colors.** Familiarize yourself with the four color perspectives: Red, blue, yellow, and green, representing different emotional states. Go back and do the exercise if you haven't.

▶ **Shifting perspectives.** Practice telling four stories about neutral objects. You can practice while driving, standing in line or make a game of it with your partner, friends or kids to develop flexibility in your perspective taking.

▶ **Build flexibility gradually.** Start Around the World Storytelling with neutral objects and progressively move to more meaningful topics. Don't rush to address the most challenging pain points; build flexibility first.

CHAPTER FIFTEEN

Not Forgetting the Obvious

"You can't stop the waves, but you can learn to surf."
JON KABAT-ZINN

I (Renée) have found peace in prescribing to this set of life instructions I received in one of my trauma training courses: Right Answer Always, Relax, RAAR. It's completely counterintuitive, but makes sense once you get it. When your body is relaxed, it's more comfortable, you think more clearly and you can live more congruently with your values and integrity because you're more connected to your executive functioning wizard brain, as opposed to being wound up in a reactionary loop of your tense body driven by your reptilian brain. It's why we encouraged you to do so many reps of pulse checks. Being aware tends to elicit a deep autonomic relaxation response. When we pay attention to our body, it will often relax. It's what they train in combat situations. When you train your body to be relaxed in the face of real and perceived danger, it's most effective for the greatest possibility of outcomes that are in alignment with your values, integrity and how you want to live your life.

There's nothing better to orient you to this moment than doing a pulse check. Pulse checks automatically induce a relaxation response in your body. Relaxing your body is always the right thing to do. You may remember from Chapter Thirteen when we presented the work of Eric Gentry, PhD and master traumatologist, who said "all you need to do" is repeat that process of intentionally relaxing your body 200 times per day.

Your body tells the truth about any given moment in the reality of here and now. If your body is too uncomfortable, then orient yourself to the objective, physical safety in your present moment environment. That will then have an effect on your body and allow you to find some safety in or around your body.

Willow trees bend better than oak trees and are less likely to get uprooted in a storm. It's the same with your nervous system. A flexible nervous system is a resilient nervous system. That's why it's key to develop a Flexibility Mindset, as opposed to a rigid mindset that keeps you stuck and not resilient to the inevitable storms and changing circumstances of your life.

In George Bonanno's book, *The End of Trauma*, his research findings present what works for being resilient in the face of adversity and trauma. His 40 years of scientific data collection has demonstrated three components that work better together than others, and they work synergistically. The three components are:

1. Possessing optimism
2. Challenge orientation
3. Confidence in coping skills

In the face of something bad happening, you may find yourself saying or thinking, "This is terrible." You wouldn't be wrong because that is accurate, valid and true for you. What's also objectively true is, if this is your only perspective, you can become stuck in a biochemical narrative which might result in an unintentional rigid mindset around what happened. This can create a self-fulfilling prophecy in your health.

I can tell you this, because I know it. Here's what I did to combat it: I wrote the words of the flexibility mindset on a sticky note. And I kept that sticky note around my kitchen sink so I would see it often and could remind myself of the new narrative I wanted to create in the face of difficult places where I was stuck in "This is terrible."

Rigid Mindset says: "This is terrible."

Flexibility Mindset says: "Okay, this terrible thing happened. I can do this. It is going to be okay. Let me just figure out what I need to do." These are literally the words I wrote down on my sticky note.

You can see in this image below that there is optimism in the "It's going to be okay." The confidence in coping is implied with "Let me just figure out what I need to do" and leads to the challenge orientation. Challenge orientation looks at terrible things with the outlook of a Challenger, as opposed to a Victim or Persecutor. The Challenger views this scenario as an opportunity to solve a problem and build more confidence in coping with life's ever changing circumstances.

If you want to stretch beyond the rigid mindset within you, there's great news. You can! Simply write some supportive words that are meaningful to you on a sticky note (you can do what I did, or create your own), read it often and repeat your new script frequently, especially if you catch yourself stuck in the "This is terrible" story! Challenge that rigid oak tree of a mindset within you and develop a strong, flexible willow tree mindset instead.

When the body freezes, it's like a lockdown—vocal cords even go silent. This impairs clear thinking and speaking up, a result of your biology, not intelligence. But there's hope: Like training a dog, you can train your body to navigate freeze responses. A patient used a green index card with strategies to manage their own freezes effectively.

Creating a resource like a green index card helps navigate overwhelm. Understanding your body's freeze signs and addressing them can ground you. Thawing frozen vocal cords through humming or singing helps regain control.

Cold showers, albeit uncomfortable, are powerful tools to reset your nervous system's response to shock. Like Jill, who initially resisted but later controlled post-concussion headaches and anxiety with cold rinses, the technique's success lies in the method used. Jill employed a graded exposure process, reshaping her nervous system's response to stress. You can learn more about her cold journey in this video interview: https://bit.ly/3UqP2qh.

A brief pit stop or "shake and shift" can also recalibrate your system. Lying down and propping up your feet checks your body's engine. Shaking or dancing helps release stress, restoring positive energy and aiding in endorphin release. Rome wasn't built in a day; changing chemical habits takes time.

Did you know that listening to music can be an effective way to promote well-being? Music has a unique ability on the brain in that it occupies significant real estate across both hemispheres. In other words, a little input of music creates a lot of change in widespread brain activity. It links your endocrine, limbic and immune systems through the HPA axis. Pleasant and unpleasant music both affect the amygdala and play a crucial role in regulating your body's responses to stress and maintaining overall health. Music has a similar effect in your amygdala and hypothalamus as the labeling exercise you did in the Three Word Checks-Ins. Scientific studies show that pleasurable music increases brain activity in regions associated with emotion and reward, while listening to unpleasant music induces the opposite effect in the brain chemistry signals in the amygdala and the hypothalamus. There are so many options and variations to promote your health with music, including binaural beats, bilateral stimulation, solfeggio frequencies, or nature sounds. Play with what elicits the best feelings in you!

By cranking up the music and letting the vibrations carry you away, you can tap into the transformative power of music and experience a new level of relaxation and emotional release. Whether you're seeking an escape from the daily grind or simply looking to boost your mood, music is a powerful tool that can help you achieve your wellness goals. So why wait? Start incorporating music into your daily routine today and discover the many benefits of this simple yet powerful action!

Aroma therapy is another good tool. You're stressed at work? Maybe you can't light up that lavender candle with your boss hovering around, but maybe you can get a small cup of peppermint tea or an essential oil and smell that throughout the day. Remember this: Small doses of goodness throughout the day pay bigger and bigger dividends the more you practice them. You are learning to change your sensory perceptions. You are changing moment by moment the inputs and in doing so, you are literally changing the way your brain is processing your environment and actively rewiring how your body connects with your brain.

Here's another one that works for some people. Journal your truth. We know, we know, we've suggested journaling previously, but it's seriously so helpful and healing! Dump out your whole truth on the pages of a notebook. How do you really feel? Don't hold back. Put it down on paper. You don't have to bottle it up anymore. Release it. Once it's down on paper, you can do what you want with it. You can save it for future reference. Or you can crumple it up and throw it away. You can bury it in the ground if you want. The important thing is by journaling you've released it from the bottled up state it was in your body. The key is that you are not a bad person for what you are feeling. These feelings aren't a reflection of your character. There is positive intention behind every feeling, but to understand that positive intention, you have to reflect on it and release it.

You can also put the tip of your tongue out. And grip it gently between your teeth. Breathe out twice. Now breathe in deeply. This regulates your system.

Or I'll use my fingers to put pressure on the palms of my hands. I'll put pressure from my fingertips on my cheeks. I'll lightly tap my fingers right under my nose. I'll put pressure from my tongue on and around the insides of my teeth, cheeks and gums. These small pressure points release enzymes throughout your body and help bring you back to the present.

Want something else? Connect with someone safe. Go get coffee with a coworker you like. Call your best friend. Snuggle with a beloved pet. Social engagement is a powerful pain reducer. It turns off the fight, flight and freeze response.

Tears, often seen as the language of the soul, hold an incredible power in the process of healing. Beyond a mere expression of sadness or pain, crying acts as a profound release mechanism, allowing emotions to flow freely. In the tender surrender of tears, the body releases stress hormones, offering a cathartic cleansing of the mind and spirit. It's in these moments of vulnerability that healing begins.

Focused breathing is important, but you've probably had people over and over again tell you to breathe deeply, and maybe you just can't. Maybe you're not a good breather, as I've heard many people self-identify. That's fine! No problem. Why don't you try not breathing for a bit. That's right. Just stop. Your body will breathe again when it's ready, and when you stop forcing it to breathe a certain way, it often takes a more life-giving inhale all on its own. Alternatively, you can focus on fully exhaling. Exhale all the way, like you're blowing out birthday candles. Then pause and let your body take the next breath on its own accord. Usually, your body will follow that deep exhale with a bigger breath than you have been able to muster on your own by forcing or "shoulding" a certain way of breathing. Your lungs naturally want to pull air in when they are fully emptied.

This one's a little bit silly. I call it Puppy Breathing. That's right. I want you to breathe like a puppy. Stick your tongue out a little and take short breaths like panting. Do some repeated sniffing, like a dog smells the side of a tree. How does that make you feel? Probably a little silly. It probably made you laugh. You know what? Silly is good. Laughter is good.

Just stop. Stop everything. Don't do anything. Give yourself permission to do nothing for 30 seconds, and see what kind of body impulse emerges. Notice what kind of movement, posture or position your body feels desire to move into or toward. Let your body do what it wants.

Do one other quick action. Stand up and take a bow. Wow, that bow just released a few healing endorphins throughout your body. I'll give you a standing ovation.

All of these techniques can be added to your toolbox and build up your repertoire of skills for greater self-efficacy. Similar to any medicine, if you don't use it, you won't see benefit from it. Anyone can acquire new skills, and they will likely experience benefit from doing so. Their perceived value may be short lived, or long lasting, or anything in between. When you strategically apply these skills, that is where the real magic starts. In other words, when you recognize in a moment of dysregulation (a DIM), and take one of these actions to re-regulate (a SIM), you are restoring control in your system. Those are moments of truth when you take your power back and upgrade the programming of your primal nervous system patterning. When you take a DIM and create a SIM, you stop your nervous system's instinctual survival-based programs from running your life. Putting these quick, little, incremental actions to work will yield big dividends.

Each of the aforementioned small steps increase dopamine, serotonin, oxytocin, and endorphins. You are flooding your system with these good hormones each time you take one of these small actions. Doing small doses throughout the day will be more effective in creating long-lasting, structural change in your nervous system. Taking 10 to 20 seconds every 20 minutes throughout your day, as opposed to 30 minutes in one sitting, will be more supportive for you during the stresses of any given day. When you sprinkle little movement snacks and baby regulation doses throughout your day, you're getting more frequent boosts of restorative, positive healing into your system. These small actions are restoring you back to equilibrium as you stay in the ups and downs of your life with all its stressors.

Embracing self-care can be an important part of managing health and finding happiness. Here are a few ways to practice self-care.

Sleep is essential for physical and mental well-being. Make sure to get enough sleep each night to help your body recover and function at its best. Aim for 7-9 hours of sleep per night to allow your body to rest and repair itself. A blinding flash of the obvious here: A good mattress and pillow can also help support your body while you sleep. Consistency in your sleep routine is crucial. Do your best to go to bed and wake up around the same time every day. Matthew Walker's book, *Sleep* is another fantastic scientific resource for learning more about how and why it's vital to optimize your sleep behaviors.

A healthy diet can help support overall physical and mental well-being, as well as help manage pain. Eat a variety of nutrient-rich foods and limit processed and sugary foods. You are what you eat. Garbage in, garbage out. There are many common expressions that relate to food. The take-home message of all of them is that the way you eat affects and reflects the way you feel.

Many people talk about how important it is to have good posture. I don't believe there is such a thing as good or bad posture. I think there are different postures and dosages of postures that can lead to optimal and less optimal states of blood flow. Please consider staying curious about which postures feel good for you, for how long, *in your lived experience*. There's no such thing as a bad posture, only postures that are held at end range for too long. This will make you feel bad because your tissues have become too ischemic and acidic.

Being overweight can put extra strain on your muscles, your confidence and self-worth. Maintaining a healthy weight may help you reduce injury and pain across the domains of your physical, emotional and social well-being.

Practice stress-relief techniques that you like and work for you. If you don't like it, you won't keep doing it. Stress can worsen pain. It's important for you to find sustainable ways to stay with practices that support you in managing both the positive and negative stress in your life. This could include relaxation techniques, such as deep breathing or meditation, or engaging in activities that you find enjoyable and stress-relieving, such as hobbies or exercise.

Boundaries are a vital part of finding peace in your life journey. They can be complicated, challenging and worth exploring. Learn more to support yourself as needed. Remove or distance unsafe people, jobs or circumstances in your life, because they feed into toxic and chronic feelings of red and blue circuits in your nervous system. Boundaries can run deep and be complex, so please consider the support of a trained professional as needed in your circumstances.

By incorporating these self-care techniques into your daily routine, you are reinforcing the belief that you are valuable and worth taking care of. This will support you in having a solid foundation and physiology to maintain greater states of health, joy and happiness.

Just like food is medicine, movement is medicine. Be sure to include frequent movement throughout your day to break up the postural monotony of whatever your work and life day ergonomics entail. Exercise that is dosed and applied for your body in whatever stage or age it is, will improve flexibility, strength and balance. Find an exercise routine that works for you and stick with it.

Exercise, like medication, has the ability to be dosed for your optimal health. Pain relievers can be taken at a dosage that will relieve your headache or kill you. Weightlifting can be dosed through varying the type of weights you lift, the intensity, the frequency, duration or repetitions. Yoga, dance, tai chi, swimming, running, rowing, skiing, basketball, pretty much any form of exercise can be considered in terms of its dosage. You want to optimize your dosage of exercise to maximize your benefits from exercise. Many people struggle with how to optimally dose exercise and need support in figuring that out. Get support. When you maintain a flexibility mindset, do movement you love and adjust exercise dosage as you age, you're more likely to become like Agnes Keleti, the 102-year-old Olympian who still taught gymnastics classes.

One way to improve strength and flexibility is through regular stretching. Stretching can help to improve range of motion and decrease muscle tension. When I began seeing Renée, she helped me significantly with simple exercises in stretching, which enabled me to be more focused and productive at work. They also supported me to sleep better and wake up rested.

The number of stretches you have been taught or can find on the internet is overwhelmingly abundant. We recommend you approach this scientifically. Pay attention to your body before and after any exercise or stretch you do. If the post exercise feeling is more good than bad, that's your body saying, "Yes, please, may I have another." It's common to have temporary discomfort during new activity, especially if you've been in pain, less mobile or had symptoms for a while. If symptoms last less than 10 minutes after any stretch, please consider them "office noise." If you have symptoms that limit your normal mobility and function for more than 1-3 days, it's likely an inflammatory response and will settle down; use the RICE (Rest, Ice, Compression, Elevation) acronym and return to a lower dose of movement next time.

For more information on specific movement practices in alignment with the culture of this book, we recommend checking out Renée's YouTube channel (@nervoussystemninja). It has numerous videos on how to develop your own Nervous System Ninja skills through various exercises, stretches, techniques, and education sessions for a stronger, more nimble nervous system. You can also reference Renée's website **https://greentreemind.com** or **https://ns-ninja.com/** to learn more.

For more information on empowerment coaching, we recommend you check out Wilene Dunn's website **www.wilenedunn.com**. Wilene is devoted to supporting you to maximize your full potential in reaching your desired results.

Gratitude is a powerful and transformative emotion that allows us to appreciate and acknowledge the positive aspects of our lives. It is the quality of being thankful and showing appreciation for the people, experiences and blessings that surround us. When we cultivate a mindset of gratitude, we shift our focus from what is lacking to what is present, fostering a sense of contentment and fulfillment.

Gratitude is powerful and transformative.

Expressing gratitude has numerous benefits for our well-being, both mentally and physically. Research has shown that practicing gratitude regularly can reduce stress, increase resilience, improve sleep quality, and enhance overall happiness. It helps us develop a more optimistic outlook on life and strengthens our relationships with others. When we express our appreciation and gratitude to others, it strengthens the bond we share with them. It deepens our connections and fosters a sense of belonging and mutual support.

In a world that often emphasizes what is lacking or what needs improvement, cultivating gratitude allows us to shift our attention to what is already abundant and positive in our lives. It reminds us to appreciate the simple joys, the acts of kindness and the beauty that surrounds us each day. Gratitude is a transformative force that can bring immense joy, contentment and fulfillment to our lives.

Occasionally, you might have resistance toward gratitude practices; you have an internal filter suggesting "you should" practice gratitude. If you have resistance around practicing gratitude, that's perfectly okay. In our experience that is coming from a place of hurt and pain that hasn't yet been healed. It is our wish, hope and prayer that you find the support, care and love you need to return to genuine circuits of appreciation.

If you happen to find yourself in a time of your life with many circumstances that are difficult to bear, finding that crack in the dam against gratitude can be a real challenge and that's okay. Start small. Appreciate the feeling of sunshine on your face. Consider reflecting and having mini celebrations. All it takes is a little crack to set in motion a new chain of chemical events within. It can take time, but research does show that in time, this practice does work.

CHAPTER REFLECTIONS

▶ **RAAR - Right Answer Always, Relax.** When faced with challenges, remember to stay calm and relaxed. What is one thing you can do when faced with a challenge to help you relax in the moment? Maintaining a relaxed state can help you make better decisions.

- ▶ **Create a toolbox of techniques** to regulate your nervous system. Experiment with various strategies like humming, shaking, cold showers, smelling pleasant scents, and connecting with safe people. Write down the ones that work for you on an index card for easy referencing.
- ▶ **Give yourself extra space, grace and compassion** when it comes to boundaries; they can be especially complex. Remember that people who don't respond well to your boundaries are those that aren't served by you having them.
- ▶ **Recognize freeze responses.** What does a freeze response look like for you? What circumstances, people or environments elicit it in your system? What helps it thaw?
- ▶ **Resilience is built** upon possessing optimism, challenge orientation and confidence in coping skills. When something feels hard, overwhelming or scary, consider saying to yourself, "This is a challenge," as opposed to, "This is hard, or I can't."

CHAPTER SIXTEEN

Love is All You Need

*"Our sorrows and wounds are healed only
when we touch them with compassion."*
BUDDHA

It's easy to sing the Beatles song, *All You Need is Love*. In our experience, it is *way* harder to live it. We can choose to get better (or not) at facing uncomfortable and difficult situations. Love is something that can help you along the way. That being said, if that is to be true, let's get clear on the definition of love we are using here so we can all be on the same page.

Love is not synonymous with pain. In its best expression, love can be a beautiful and transformative force that brings joy, understanding and growth. However, it is unfortunate that some individuals have, from an early age, associated love with abuse, neglect and suffering. If your own perception has been shaped by this painful understanding, we find it genuinely heartbreaking that your experiences have led you to believe that love is inherently painful.

We believe that it is for you to explore how you define love and how your nervous system defines love. Oxford Dictionary defines love as "an intense feeling of affection." We'd like to expand upon this definition of love here.

Please consider the following thought expirement: Imagine an eight-lane highway with no dividers or clear delineations on what direction traffic should be going, nor with any clarity on what speed. Cars going anywhere and everywhere with no order, screaming and yelling with a terrifying feeling of playing real life bumper cars. Obviously this is an exercise in your imagination, but you could see how this would be a clear recipe for confusion and frustration at best, disaster and tragedy at worst.

In our opinion, this is exactly what western civilization is doing when we only use one word for love. Perhaps you might consider our invitation to be inspired by how the ancient Greeks actually used eight different words for love. Learning more about these eight words can change your life. It is beyond the scope of this book to deeply explore this concept, but we offer this brief synopsis here for you:

1. Eros, or sexual passion.
2. Philia, or deep friendship.
3. Ludus, or playful love.
4. Agape, or love for everyone.
5. Pragma, or longstanding love.
6. Philautia, or love of the self.
7. Storge, or familiar/family love.
8. Mania, or obsessive love.

When these eight lanes of love are not understood and kept clear in one's own psyche, trouble can arise. A few extreme examples could include when eros is confused with family love and incest occurs. Or when one person experiences mania toward someone who only feels agape toward them, the extreme possession can lead to the necessity of a restraining order. A more benign, yet equally painful expression, is when you feel only ludus toward someone, but they feel eros in return. This can create a lot of confusion and torture within the heart of a human soul and its longing. If you are clear on the type of love you feel toward another and have the ability to communicate that effectively, you will save yourself and others from a whole lot of heartbreak.

For me (Renée), I do better with a working definition of thinking that love is a behavior and a choice we can make. Our choices can lead to feelings that vary from high to low in their pleasantness. For example, I didn't feel intensely pleasant feelings of love when I was picking up 34 piles of puppy poop on my bedroom carpet, surrounded by different smells including doggie diarrhea, various cleaning chemicals and cold winter air from the bedroom window. Yet as I was on my hands and knees scrubbing at two in the morning, something in me *knew* that *this* is what love is.

Another time, I had intense abdominal pain as a six-year-old, sitting in the passenger seat of my mom's car while she was driving. My mom in her desperate attempt to make me feel better, said to me, "Just go!" The shock of her suggestion to actually alleviate my pain by relieving my bowels in that moment (in my pants!!!) was utterly horrifying to me. In fact, her words ironically stopped my painful fecal urgency dead in its tracks. I can't imagine it would feel pleasant, good or loving to help clean up your six-year-old's diarrhea, but her willingness to do so in that moment spoke unconditional acceptance of all that I am. Her all-conditional acceptance of me through her words that day included the acceptance of all my biological expressions, including potential fecal matter on the fabric of her passenger side seat! That's a powerful kind of love in my experience. What she was saying to me was, "I don't care if you need to take a dump in my car, do whatever you need to in order to feel better."

I (Wilene) have a working definition of love that includes acceptance of what is. Meaning, accepting all the colors in another person, and accepting all of them in yourself. That doesn't necessarily mean you'll choose to continue interacting with another person and all of their colors, but allowing all colors to exist without making them wrong certainly brings about a lot more peace. This is a very loving thing to do and also corresponds well with the I Corinthians 13 definition of love:

> "Love is patient, love is kind. It does not envy, it does not boast, it is not proud. It does not dishonor others, it is not self-seeking, it is not easily angered, it keeps no record of wrongs. Love does not delight in evil but rejoices with the truth. It always protects, always trusts, always hopes, always perseveres. Love never fails. And now these three remain: Faith, hope and love. But the greatest of these is love."

I (Renée) also prescribe, when it comes to love, that it is a good idea to put your own oxygen mask on first, at least when you're interacting with other non-dependent humans older than the age of eight. Take action and acceptance toward finding the circuits of safety within your own nervous system first. The more you do that, the more you are contributing to a world with greater regulation in our collective nervous system. And seriously, this way is easier said than done!

Through writing this chapter, we explored how perceptions of love from the past can influence present experiences of love and that our perceptions can be updated. This is such good news! For example, I (Wilene) explored love from the perspective of a past relationship where my partner was so incredibly red all the time and that did not work with my nervous system because I was taught from a very young age that red (anger, frustration, annoying, pissed off) was wrong. Growing up, my dad was very red, and I ended up in a lot of red relationships. My family dynamic was that my dad was wrong for being red/angry all the time and I believe he was pretty stuck in red. When I got into a red relationship with a partner that was incredibly angry and annoyed most of the time, I made my partner wrong. Now as I look back and have put into practice all Renée and I have experienced through the writing of this book, I am convinced that Love is All We Need. The kind of love that allows for the red and the blue and the green and the yellow. Love for all four colors of our nervous system. I expressed that now, if I could go back, I would embrace the red in my partner. I would be more inquisitive to the red and find out the story of the blue, green and yellow which is a loving act of kindness for ourselves in our story and for others in their stories.

I was watching a movie recently where one of the characters was a writer and her co-star in the film was the main character in her books. They go through a journey that puts them in a few places where they have to make a decision and the main character says, "It's your story, how do you want to write it?" This life is your story (remember the shift out of Victim is into Creator), how do *you* want to write it? If you knew you could write the outcome to your story, how would you write it?

Let's all agree that a shared working definition of love is one that activates circuits of safety and connection. Let's explore the relationship that love has with healing. We believe the most powerful force in your life that can help you heal from pain is love—love for yourself, love for others and love from others. Love is a force and power that we may not fully comprehend, but it does seem to be connected, having an effective impact on healing.

Lorimer Moseley, a neuroscientist with over 180 peer-reviewed scientific journals, was asked the following question during a radio interview: "What would you most want to research, if you were given five million dollars to solve any problem in the world?"

Here is a paraphrase of Dr. Moseley's response:

"I would love to find out the best way to convince everyone that they are both loved and loving. If we could do that, we would drastically reduce stuff like chronic pain. To love and be loved is probably the strongest biological drive. I would imagine that if any human could be absolutely convinced that they are physically safe from everything, they will not experience pain."

Think about it. Love truly is the most powerful healing force there is. There is nothing that compares to the powerful dynamic that comes from loving and being loved in return. Nothing can transform your body or your mind like love. Nothing can make you feel safe like love. Love is a powerful antidote to the pain you experience, as you hopefully earlier collected in the 3D Perspective Taking exercise of this book.

In the physical dimension of pain, the healing touch of a loved one eases tension. Love is the opposite of negative stress. More importantly, oxytocin, which is released through loving physical touch, is literally wired into our chemical makeup. When we cuddle, when we touch the legs of loved ones at night, when we caress a favorite pet, our bodies receive a huge dose of oxytocin, also called the love hormone. As oxytocin floods our system, it acts as a neurotransmitter in the brain. The neurotransmitters in our brain are powerful and not to be underestimated. The endogenous chemicals in our brain can be 50 times more powerful than any drug on the market!

My (Renée) nervous system had a difficult time adjusting from a rapid change in my family of six, to a family of two. My mom had died, my older sisters launched to live their adult lives and my dad was struggling in a dazed depression that felt like a Pig Pen meets Eeyore cloud of pain dust that touched everything at home. Household snuggles, playful wrestling and physical touch were insufficient. Once I tried to hug my dad after a hard day when he came home from work; his arms fell limp and heartbreakingly lifeless to his side.

Thankfully, I have a memory that alleviates and lightens the load of that heavy burden as it was stored in my body. I remember feeling a break from the Eeyore cloud one night, when a priest from Mexico came over for dinner. At one point during the evening, Father David gave me a hug while all three of us stood in the kitchen. It felt like I had escaped the heavy, dark cloud and snuck into a little pocket of peace where I had relief from the heavy emotional pain that saturated me. I can feel the comfort of that priest's care that seemed to radiate from his body and activate my circuits of joy and feelings of pleasant love, even as I write these words from an event over 30 years ago. Oxytocin works, and it can be long lasting if we choose to remember and focus on the moments when we receive it.

Healing and love are contagious.

Your body can be an annoying truth teller that will communicate honestly with you, where you still carry circuits of incomplete stress responses and 3D pain inside your nervous system. The first part of healing through love is to become conscious of the unconscious.

After your hurts have been seen, heard and understood in a more 3D fashion, it's time to engage the second part of healing through love: Rewriting your story.

When Wilene and I were 3D processing my headache and gut pain, she acted as a Challenger to my uni-dimensional, monochromatic blue, "I'm broken and I can't heal" Victim story. Wilene asked me, "In all the stories that you can tell about your life, all the multiple thousands and trillions of stories, why would you choose to hold onto the one where you were a Victim, feeling abandoned, rejected, terrified, and fearful of being alone? Why would you go back and choose the loss of your mother? Out of the billions of stories we all can choose, why does anyone choose the stories they are choosing?"

When Wilene asked me why I chose that Victim story, I watched myself become rather defensive from my red perception of "her attack." I said, "First of all, I'm not choosing it. My nervous system was perceiving distress accurately according to the subconscious, red and blue body circuitry it was stuck in below the conscious screen of my awareness. Second, my gut has been holding that story *because it hasn't been loved enough.* Once that story has been loved enough, only then can I take all these broken pieces of myself, glue them back together with love, and then put that story on a shelf." As Brene Brown says, "Owning our story can be challenging but not nearly as difficult as spending our lives running from it. Embracing our vulnerabilities is risky but not nearly as dangerous as giving up on love and belonging and joy—the experiences that make us the most vulnerable. Only when we are brave enough to explore the darkness will we discover the infinite power of our light."

I was able to more deeply heal my story and tap into its infinite power of light on a deeper level through the context of writing this book and having my gut-brain blow a big fat bubble of pain in the final chapter. Without the healing power of that pain I would have not been enable to heal a deeper layer of my own story.

Why do you get caught up in loops of telling the same old body-mind-life story? Why does that happen? We believe it is because the wounding in your old story hasn't healed. The places you are still hurt from the past haven't been loved enough. Or perhaps you haven't yet had access to the courage and vulnerability to open yourself up to receive the love. Hurt and pain are not easy to open up to, nor are they easy to love. Loving one another as fellow human beings through all the painful places within us isn't easy. Thankfully, humans are more resilient and stronger than we know. Our system has access to more powers of healing in our humanity than we are even aware of.

The hidden genius of you retelling the same old wounded story is that your system is trying to flag you (or anyone who will pay attention) to get its needs met. That painful story in you wants to be seen, heard and loved enough so you can get back into your wholeness as a complete human being. Now you have a choice: Do you want to listen to your body and its stories in a one or three dimensional kind of way? Do you want to stay frustrated and limited by continuing to use ineffective, one-dimensional solutions to solve your three-dimensional problems? Do you want to tell your core stories in a way that makes you feel trapped or as though your body was a powerful teacher that helped you learn how to tell your core stories as though they matter, can heal and have a significant place in your life? All your stories matter and are meaningful. You can learn to experience them in ways that hurt or help you. What if you switched the story you were telling and found a new way to tell that old story, or tell a different story altogether? You have the ability to find a new story about your old story that reframes your current now.

It was the love in Wilene's challenge, my willingness to be open even though I was feeling hurt and angry, and applying my "Around the World Storytelling" skills that enabled me to experience other colors in my abandonment story. I felt safe and supported to break free and build new neural pathways inside of me. It was the power of human love, the agape that was being exchanged through mutual stories of pain, that allowed us both to rewrite another layer of our old stories and create something new.

It wasn't until the writing of this book, a completely different context, and being seen by Wilene, that I was able to see how the way I was telling this story, in that particular way and color, was creating physical distress and relational discomfort in my life. Wilene and I were talking and she said:

"We don't want to forget those significant things that moved us forward, and we also don't want to forget about all the other stories and perspectives that move us forward, the loving, healing and fun stories.

So you decided that this story is the important one. We get to decide that, right?"

Don't mistake pockets of pain for a world of hurt. I had forgotten who I was and that my system was capable of healing. I had become disconnected from the original design of my human goodness. I had forgotten that tissues heal, and so do people. The love I experienced through Wilene challenging my story acted as medicine for me to help me remember who I am and to remind me that humans can heal.

Don't mistake pockets of pain for a world of hurt.

Our natural state is a flexible nervous system that has the ability to shift perspectives and see any given circumstance from all four colors. You may realize that your symptoms may or may not ever go away permanently—life will always have changing circumstances that can include problems we don't want to have. As we build our confidence to cope with challenges and have a degree of confidence in our ability to solve them and deal with them as they emerge, it gives us a greater sense of control over and within ourselves, our minds, bodies and lives.

Please consider this an invitation and an encouragement to take action and go do things that make you feel more alive. Even if it's one tiny moment at a time. Don't wait for some external magic bullet to come along and make your life feel better. Take a tiny action, one moment at a time. Each micro moment of feeling a bit better as a result of an action you took will help. You can and will heal your life along the way with your tools and a good support system.

Many hesitate to take action because they don't necessarily know where they're going or what lies ahead. Please take action anyway. There will always be unknowns in your life path ahead and waiting for them to go away will stall you out for life. Healing isn't a clear, linear or straightforward path that you can always see or know what's coming. The path towards healing *is* available for you (even if it doesn't feel like it sometimes), and love (in the form of safety and connection) is the vehicle that will get you there. Skills you learned in this book will help a lot."

You are ultimately responsible for your life and all that is in it now. That doesn't mean that bad things are your fault, and it doesn't mean you are to blame. Sometimes, bad things just happen and it's not because you manifested them. Taking a stand of radical responsibility for your life is a powerful and brave act, and it also requires radical compassion for yourself and others. Taking responsibility for your own lived experience is not always easy, but the squeeze is certainly worth the juice it provides.

Love, pain, traffic jams, swarms of bees, and schools of fish all have one thing in common: They don't follow logical rules. They are all emergent expressions of consciousness. But you can learn to recognize and develop greater pattern recognition. And you can learn to believe that there is a benevolent force within you that wants to help you on this wild and difficult path toward healing and happiness.

I (Renée) like to call one expression of this internal healing voice your BIT, or your Benevolent Inner Therapist. One day, a patient shared a story of how he was seething angry about a long grocery store line when all of a sudden he heard a clear voice say, "You are responsible for how you feel." He looked behind him to see if anyone had said that, yet no one was there. We decided that he's not delusional, but rather, he's apparently got a BIT that wanted to help him out when he was lost in an internal cloud of seeing red. It was exactly the spontaneous internal cue he needed to remember to do a few calming exercises, and then feel 50% more calm. It was the same BIT voice within that reminded another patient of mine while rumbling with anxiety during a tense phone call, that the voice on the other end of the line "is not dangerous right now." This cue reminded her to take a breath, settle herself and finish the call with clarity. Healing is not a straight line. It's emergent and unpredictable, but it does happen.

#HealingHappens

We thank you for the gift of connection and for the power of the written word. May our writing be a testimony to your goodness and a source of inspiration to all who read it.

CHAPTER REFLECTIONS

- ▸ **Be open to the possibility** of love showing up in unexpected ways. Can you think of a time when love and support came from places and people you didn't expect?
- ▸ **Healing is contagious.** Just as negative emotions can be contagious, healing experiences and love can also spread. Witnessing other's healing journeys can trigger your own sense of healing.
- ▸ **Be curious instead of furious** when faced with emotional or physical pain. Approach it with curiosity rather than anger. If you stayed open to challenging sensations, what difference would it make in your body? Would that difference facilitate or hinder healing for you?
- ▸ **Engage in radical responsibility.** Take responsibility for your own healing journey. Think of a time when you demonstrated the power to rewrite a story and shift your perspective.
- ▸ **On some level** you are both Loved and Loving. Say that out loud, "I am Loved and Loving." Notice how this possibility penetrates circuits of fear, threat, protect, and defend, and find healing through your Authentic Self.

Epilogue

In the spirit of appreciation, I, (Wilene) would like to share some final thoughts. Working with Renée on the book, *Getting My Happy Back*, has been a truly wonderful experience. From the moment we began collaborating, I could feel her love, kindness and dedication to helping others. She has a unique ability to help others feel safe and supported, and it has been a pleasure to share this journey with her. I am deeply grateful for the opportunity to work together on this book, and I have no doubt that it will be a valuable resource for countless people looking to improve their health and overall well-being. Renée is a true professional and a kind soul. I feel fortunate to have had the opportunity to collaborate with her.

My final thought for *Getting My Happy Back* is the powerful impact that shifting our focus from negative conditions to positive desires can have on our lives. I have shared my own experience of how focusing on what I wanted, rather than dwelling on my pain and other negative conditions, helped me make significant changes in my life.

I believe that this shift in focus is crucial for anyone looking to make positive changes, whether it's in your physical health or any other aspect of your life. When you focus on what you want, you open yourself up to new possibilities and opportunities. You become more curious and open to learning and trying new things. On the other hand, when you focus on negative conditions, pains and frustrations, you can become stuck in a cycle of negativity and despair.

It is important to stay focused on your path, rather than getting sidetracked by distractions or obstacles. It's all too easy to become sidetracked and lose sight of our goals. By staying focused on what we want, we are more likely to stay on track and achieve our desired outcomes.

I (Renée) believe that tissues can heal and trauma can end. Not just because I am a hopeful dreamer, but because scientific data tells me that is possible. I am deeply grateful for David Butler, Adrian Louw, and George Bonanno; without these three gentlemen and their scientific research endeavors, I would have never believed that healing can happen. I have deep respect and regard for my co-author, Wilene Dunn. Her supportive presence through our writing has been healing for wounds within me deeper than my cognitive capacities can go. Because she stood by and witnessed me through the ups and downs of writing this book, I found courage within to access and share my authentic voice. This book is a reflection of my gratitude and contribution toward supporting us all in getting closer to the reality that healing can happen.

Listening is one part. Allowing and accepting is another. I learned on a deep level through this creative process with Wilene how to truly be with and accept every color in my nervous system. The broken, hateful, scared, and ugly parts of me are so grateful to Wilene as she taught me how to love those circuits within me more. There's nothing quite like being thrown into the arena to learn how to rumble.

Lastly, we are grateful for you, the reader, the learner and the committed human to living well. Thank you for sharing your precious time with us to discover our perspectives on a path that can help you get more of your happy back. We wish you beauty, safety, goodness, truth, and an abundance of resourcing and support along your way. Many times, it will feel like you're alone. And you may be. But on some plane of existence, we believe that you are never alone. We think that's so important that we'll say it again: No matter what you may be thinking or feeling, you're not alone.

One of the keys to getting your happy back is about the power of focus and how you can use it to make positive change in your life. When you shift your attention toward what you want, stay focused on your desired outcome and do what it takes to get there, you can overcome any obstacle. It's okay to get off track. I find comfort in remembering that 96% of a space shuttle's journey to the moon is course correction. In other words, 96% of the time the shuttle is off track from its target, yet still somehow reaches its destination. Set your intention, do your best to focus on your desired outcome and remember that being off course is a natural and necessary part of the process to reaching your destination.

Authenticity can hold the power to heal trauma. When you bravely open yourself to receiving love, its transformative embrace becomes the balm that restores and nourishes your wounded soul. Do whatever makes your heart sing!

References

Chapter One: It's Not You — It's Your Nervous System

1. Frank JM, Harris JD, Erickson BJ, Slikker W 3rd, Bush-Joseph CA, Salata MJ, Nho SJ. Prevalence of Femoroacetabular Impingement Imaging Findings in Asymptomatic Volunteers: A Systematic Review. Arthroscopy. 2015 Jun;31(6):1199-204. doi: 10.1016/j.arthro.2014.11.042. Epub 2015 Jan 28. PMID: 25636988.

2. Girish G, Lobo LG, Jacobson JA, Morag Y, Miller B, Jamadar DA. Ultrasound of the shoulder: asymptomatic findings in men. AJR Am J Roentgenol. 2011 Oct;197(4):W713-9. doi: 10.2214/AJR.11.6971. PMID: 21940544.

3. Nakashima H, Yukawa Y, Suda K, Yamagata M, Ueta T, Kato F. Abnormal findings on magnetic resonance images of the cervical spines in 1211 asymptomatic subjects. Spine (Phila Pa 1976). 2015 Mar 15;40(6):392-8. doi: 10.1097/BRS.0000000000000775. PMID: 25584950.

4. Brinjikji W, Luetmer PH, Comstock B, Bresnahan BW, Chen LE, Deyo RA, Halabi S, Turner JA, Avins AL, James K, Wald JT, Kallmes DF, Jarvik JG. Systematic literature review of imaging features of spinal degeneration in asymptomatic populations. AJNR Am J Neuroradiol. 2015 Apr;36(4):811-6. doi: 10.3174/ajnr.A4173. Epub 2014 Nov 27. PMID: 25430861; PMCID: PMC4464797.

5. Culvenor AG, Øiestad BE, Hart HF, Stefanik JJ, Guermazi A, Crossley KM. Prevalence of knee osteoarthritis features on magnetic resonance imaging in asymptomatic uninjured adults: a systematic review and meta-analysis. Br J Sports Med. 2019 Oct;53(20):1268-1278. doi: 10.1136/bjsports-2018-099257. Epub 2018 Jun 9. PMID: 29886437; PMCID: PMC6837253.

6. Symeonidis PD, Iselin LD, Simmons N, Fowler S, Dracopoulos G, Stavrou P. Prevalence of interdigital nerve enlargements in an asymptomatic population.

Foot Ankle Int. 2012 Jul;33(7):543-7. doi: 10.3113/FAI.2012.0543. PMID: 22835390.

7. O'Neil J, McDonald E, Chapman T, Casper D, Shakked R, Pedowitz D. Anterior Talofibular Ligament Abnormalities on Routine Magnetic Resonance Imaging of the Ankle. Foot & Ankle Orthopaedics. 2017;2(3). doi:10.1177/2473011417S000311

Chapter Two: Perception and Your Nervous System

1. Doss, A. (2018), Wording wisely: Including prevalence data and evidence based clinical outcomes of spinal and musculoskeletal degeneration in radiology reports. J Med Imaging Radiat Oncol, 62: 599-604. https://doi-org. colorado.idm.oclc.org/10.1111/1754-9485.12751

2. F. Benedetti, M. Lanotte, L. Lopiano, L. Colloca, When words are painful: Unraveling the mechanisms of the nocebo effect, Neuroscience, Volume 147, Issue 2, 2007, Pages 260-271. https://doi.org/10.1016/j. neuroscience.2007.02.020.

Chapter Three: Pain Isn't — and Is — What You Think

1. Barreto RPG, Braman JP, Ludewig PM, Ribeiro LP, Camargo PR. Bilateral magnetic resonance imaging findings in individuals with unilateral shoulder pain. Journal of Shoulder and Elbow Surgery. 2019;28:1699-1706.

2. Butler D, Moseley L. Explain Pain (2nd Ed). Orthopedic Physical Therapy Products. Minneapolis, MN. 2013.

3. Elkholy AR, Farid AM, Shamhoot EA. Spontaneous Resorption of Herniated Lumbar Disk: Observational Retrospective Study in 9 Patients. World Neurosurgery. 2019;124:e453-e459.

4. Johnson MI (2017) Trauma and Pain: A Fragile Link. J Trauma Treat 6: 378. doi:10.4172/2167-1222.1000378

5. Fisher JP, Hassan DT, O'Connor N (1995) Minerva. BMJ 310: 70

6. Zhong M, Liu J, Jiang H, et al. Incidence of Spontaneous Resorption of Lumbar Disc Herniation: A Meta-Analysis. Pain physician. 2017;20:E45.

7. Schwartzberg R, Reuss BL, Burkhart BG, Butterfield M, Wu JY, McLean KW. High Prevalence of Superior Labral Tears Diagnosed by MRI in Middle-Aged Patients With Asymptomatic Shoulders. Orthopaedic Journal of Sports Medicine. 2016;4:2325967115623212-2325967115623212.

8. Vahedi H, Aalirezaie A, Azboy I, Daryoush T, Shahi A, Parvizi J. Acetabular Labral Tears Are Common in Asymptomatic Contralateral Hips With Femoroacetabular Impingement. CLINICAL ORTHOPAEDICS AND RELATED RESEARCH. 2019;477:974-979.

9. Chan BY, Allen H, Davis KW, Blankenbaker DG. MR Imaging of the hip: Avoiding pitfalls, identifying normal variants. Applied Radiology. 2018;47:8-14.

10. Bedson J, Croft P. The discordance between clinical and radiographic knee osteoarthritis: A systematic search and summary of the literature. BMC MUSCULOSKELETAL DISORDERS. 2008;9:116-116.

11. Hochreiter B, Hess S, Moser L, Hirschmann MT, Amsler F, Behrend H. Healthy knees have a highly variable patellofemoral alignment: a systematic review. Knee Surgery, Sports Traumatology, Arthroscopy. 2019:1-9.

12. Brinjikji W, Luetmer PH, Comstock B, Bresnahan BW, Chen LE, Deyo RA, Halabi S, Turner JA, Avins AL, James K, Wald JT, Kallmes DF, Jarvik JG. Syste

13. Alaiti RK, Reis FJJ. Pain in Athletes: Current Knowledge and Challenges. Int J Sports Phys Ther. 2022 Oct 1;17(6):981-983. doi: 10.26603/001c.37675. PMID: 36237643; PMCID: PMC9528677.

14. Gregg, J., Silberstein, M., Schneider, T. et al. Sonographic and MRI evaluation of the plantar plate: a prospective study. Eur Radiol 16, 2661–2669 (2006). https://doi-org.colorado.idm.oclc.org/10.1007/s00330-006-0345-8

15. Bergman AG, Fredericson M, Ho C, Matheson GO. Asymptomatic tibial stress reactions: MRI detection and clinical follow-up in distance runners. AJR Am J Roentgenol. 2004 Sep;183(3):635-8. doi: 10.2214/ajr.183.3.1830635. PMID: 15333349.

16. Saxena A, Luhadiya A, Ewen B, Goumas C. Magnetic resonance imaging and incidental findings of lateral ankle pathologic features with asymptomatic ankles. J Foot Ankle Surg. 2011 Jul-Aug;50(4):413-5. doi: 10.1053/j. jfas.2011.03.011. Epub 2011 May 12. PMID: 21570324.

17. Owens et al. Morton's neuroma: Clinical testing and imaging in 76 feet, compared to a control group. Foot and Ankle Surgery 17. September 3, 2011.

18. Lohman, M., Kivisaari, A., Vehmas, T. et al. MRI abnormalities of foot and ankle in asymptomatic, physically active individuals. Skeletal Radiol 30, 61–66 (2001). https://doi-org.colorado.idm.oclc.org/10.1007/s002560000316

19. Noback, P. C., Freibott, C. E., Tantigate, D., Jang, E., Greisberg, J. K., Wong, T., & Vosseller, J. T. (2018). Prevalence of Asymptomatic Achilles Tendinosis. Foot & Ankle International, 39(10), 1205–1209. https://doi. org/10.1177/1071100718778592

20. Melissa M. Galli, Nicole M. Protzman, Eiran M. Mandelker, Amit D. Malhotra, Edward Schwartz, Stephen A. Brigido, Examining the Relation of Osteochondral Lesions of the Talus to Ligamentous and Lateral Ankle Tendinous Pathologic Features: A Comprehensive MRI Review in an Asymptomatic Lateral Ankle Population, The Journal of Foot and Ankle Surgery, Volume 53, Issue 4, 2014, Pages 429-433, ISSN 1067-2516,

21. https://doi.org/10.1053/j.jfas.2014.03.014.

22. Melissa M. Galli, Nicole M. Protzman, Scott T. Bleazey, Stephen A. Brigido,

23. Role of Demineralized Allograft Subchondral Bone in the Treatment of Shoulder Lesions of the Talus: Clinical Results With Two-Year Follow-Up, The Journal of Foot and Ankle Sur

24. Samartin-Veiga N, Pidal-Miranda M, González-Villar AJ, et al. Transcranial direct current stimulation of three cortical targets is no more effective than placebo as treatment for fibromyalgia: a double-blind sham-controlled clinical trial. Pain. Published online September 23, 2021. doi:10.1097/j.pain.0000000000002493

25. Moseley G.L., 2007, 'Reconceptualising pain according to modern pain science', Physical Therapy Reviews 12(3), 169–178.

26. Moseley G.L. & Butler D.S., 2017, Explain pain supercharged, NOI Group Publishers, Adelaide.

27. Moseley GL, Arntz A, 2007 'The context of a noxious stimulus affects the pain it evokes', PAIN®, Volume 133, Issues 1–3, Pages 64-71.

Chapter Four: Preparing for Transformation

1. https://sphweb.bumc.bu.edu/otlt/mph-modules/sb/behavioralchangetheories/behavioralchangetheories6.html

2. Berry, M. P., Lutz, J., Schuman-Olivier, Z., Germer, C., Pollak, S., Edwards, R. R., ... & Napadow, V. (2020). Brief Self-Compassion Training Alters Neural Responses to Evoked Pain for Chronic Low Back Pain: A Pilot Study. Pain Medicine. [link to study]

3. Lutz, J., Berry, M. P., Napadow, V., Germer, C., Pollak, S., Gardiner, P., ... & Schuman-Olivier, Z. (2020). Neural activations during self-related processing in patients with chronic pain and effects of a brief self-compassion training–A pilot study. Psychiatry Research: Neuroimaging, 304, 111155. [link to study]

Chapter Seven: Identity and Human Needs

1. https://www.youtube.com/watch?v=l3bynimi8HQ

2. Maté, Gabor and Maté, Daniel. The Myth of Normal: Trauma, Illness, and Healing in a Toxic Culture. Avery Publications, 2022.

Chapter Eight: Nonviolent Communication and Unmet Needs

1. https://www.newscientist.com/article/mg23931880-400-lifting-the-lid-on-the-unconscious/

2. Leaf CM, Louw B, and Uys I. The Development of a Model for Geodesic Learning: The Geodesic Information Processing Model. Die Suid-Afrikaanse Tydskrif vir Kommunikasieafwykings, Vol 4, 1997.

3. Leaf, Caroline. Cleaning Up Your Mental Mess. Baker Books, 2021.

Chapter Nine: DIMs, SIMs and Pulse Checks

1. Sparacino J. Blood pressure, stress, and mental health. Nurs Res. 1982 Mar-Apr;31(2):89-94. PMID: 6764659.

2. Benson, Herbert. The Relaxation Response. William Morrow & Company, 2000.

3. Butler D and Moseley GL. The Explain Pain Handbook: Protectometer. Adelaide, Noigroup Publications, 2015.

Chapter Ten: STRESS RESPONSES

1. Felitti, V. J., Anda, R. F., Nordenberg, D., Williamson, D. F., Spitz, A. M., Edwards, V., Koss, M. P., & Marks, J. S. (1998). Relationship of childhood abuse and household dysfunction to many of the leading causes of death in adults: The Adverse Childhood Experiences (ACE) Study. American Journal of Preventive Medicine, 14(4), 245–258.

Chapter Twelve: The Mood Meter and Your Four Selves

1. Torre JB, Lieberman MD (2018-03-20). "Putting Feelings Into Words: Affect Labeling as Implicit Emotion Regulation". Emotion Review. 10 (2): 116–124. doi:10.1177/1754073917742706. ISSN 1754-0739. S2CID 46664580.

Chapter Thirteen: A Deeper Dive into Pulse Checks

1. Torre, J. B., & Lieberman, M. D. (2018). Putting Feelings Into Words: Affect Labeling as Implicit Emotion Regulation. Emotion Review, 10(2), 116–124. https://doi.org/10.1177/1754073917742706

2. Voss, C. (2021) "The Black Swan Group Negotiation 9."

3. Voss, C. (2021) Masterclass.

Chapter Fifteen: Not Forgetting the Obvious

1. Gentry, Eric. Forward Facing Trauma Therapy: Healing the Moral Wound. Compassion, Unlimited, 2016.

2. Arjmand HA, Hohagen J, Paton B, Rickard NS. Emotional Responses to Music: Shifts in Frontal Brain Asymmetry Mark Periods of Musical Change. Front Psychol. 2017 Dec 4;8:2044. doi: 10.3389/fpsyg.2017.02044. PMID: 29255434; PMCID: PMC5723012.

3. Greater Good Science Center at UC Berkeley (2018). The Science of Gratitude [White paper]. https://ggsc.berkeley.edu/images/uploads/GGSC-JTF_White_Paper-Gratitude-FINAL.pdf?_ga=2.149552820.309795367.1690908675-1164881034.1690908675

4. Y. Joel Wong, Jesse Owen, Nicole T. Gabana, Joshua W. Brown, Sydney McInnis, Paul Toth & Lynn Gilman (2018) Does gratitude writing improve the mental health of psychotherapy clients? Evidence from a randomized controlled trial, Psychotherapy Research, 28:2, 192-202, DOI: 10.1080/10503307.2016.1169332

Chapter Sixteen: Love is All You Need

1. "The Nature of Pain" (2011) YouTube of ABC FM Classics Margaret Throsby interview with Lorimer Moseley.

2. https://www.youtube.com/watch?v=6o_pB2AVuMI